Pra

HOW TO BE ALRIGHT UNTIL MR. RIGHT COMES ALONG

Dr. Vera McIntyre's latest book, **"How To Be Alright Until Mr. Right Comes Along"** is a much needed guide to help individuals navigate through the ups and downs of life as it relates to relationships. So many women believe that they are not whole unless they are married or in a relationship and therefore they miss out on so much that life has to offer. In **"How To Be Alright Until Mr. Right Comes Along"**, **Vera** provides proven strategies and Godly wisdom to help you become whole and happy as you proceed on your life's journey. I highly recommend this book!

_____ Dr. Rosalind Y. L. Tompkins, Author of "What Is It", "You Are Beautiful", "Rare Anointing" and "As Long As There Is Breath In Your Body, There Is Hope", Founder and Senior Pastor of Turning Point International Church, Founder and President of Mothers In Crisis, Inc.

Dr. McIntyre's book, How To Be Alright Until Mr. Right Comes Along, will inspire women of all ages, socioeconomic groups, relationship statuses, and levels of spirituality to first develop a relationship with God and then, seek His counsel, regarding matters of the heart. Dr. McIntyre encourages us to love God and love ourselves, so that we will be better equipped to love our husbands and our children.

This book is a must read for anyone who desires or knows someone who desires to have a happy, fulfilled life in her singleness while God is preparing her, and her mate, to receive His promises.

__ Dr. Natosha D. Canty, MD

A very entertaining and interesting book! I really enjoyed the ideas, inspirations, advice and instruction!

__ Nettie Thomas Black, Educator & Community Leader

HOW TO BE

Alright

UNTIL

MR. RIGHT

COMES ALONG

DR. VERA MCINTYRE

authorHOUSE®

AuthorHouse™ LLC
1663 Liberty Drive
Bloomington, IN 47403
www.authorhouse.com
Phone: 1-800-839-8640

Unless otherwise noted, Scripture quotations are taken from The Holy Bible, King James Version.

Published by AuthorHouse   08/07/2014

ISBN: 978-1-4969-1609-9 (sc)
ISBN: 978-1-4969-1608-2 (e)

Library of Congress Control Number: 2014909745

CONTENTS

DEDICATION

This book is dedicated to my daughters, Sharica, Khalilah and Andrea Hayes. My granddaughter, Jonilah Paris Megie, always holds a very special place in my heart. I pray daily for these beautiful awesome women of God. My prayer is that God blesses them with God fearing men in their lives. Until God blesses them with a significant other, my desire is that they will be alright until Mr. Right comes along.

The word "thanks" does not do justice in expressing my gratitude and appreciation, but I will try. Thank God for allowing me the opportunity to write this book. I thank my mom for introducing me to God and Christ at an early age.

A special thanks to my aunt, Nettie Thomas Black, for reading the draft in its entirety. Thanks for seeing the message and honoring it to professional quality. Thank you for your editorial insight.

To my sisters everywhere who have suffered in silence, you are not alone. My desire is that every woman be blessed until Mr. Right comes alone. I hope women all over the world grow to be all God wants them to be. I sincerely hope each woman whose eyes focus on the pages of this book be blessed to not only welcome Mr. Right but also become empowered to be **Ms. Right.**

I am absolutely sure that when women are blessed by this book, men will also be blessed. Men will gain help meets who are empowered to be the best they can be. Women and men empowered will generate stronger individuals, families, communities, states, nations and a stronger world.

INTRODUCTION

About twenty years ago, an associate of mine told me that I have a "disarming personality." For a long time, I often wondered about the meaning of this comment. I have now learned what he meant about my "disarming personality." God has positioned me to be used as an instrument for others to open up, explore, and share their deepest innermost thoughts, beliefs, feelings and fears. This "disarming personality" has open up the opportunity for many people to reveal to me their inner thoughts and emotions.

As I live and experience many of life's "mountain and valley" experiences, I have witnessed many people- old, young, males and females- come to me sharing their experiences often asking for counsel, advice and direction. Once, I was surprised by how many individuals felt comfortable sharing with me.

I have often encountered conversations with young and mature women who struggle with life issues relating to their male/female experiences or relationships. I now know that God's anointing also moves individuals to tell me about their "mountain and valley" experiences.

I hope this book, How to Be Alright Until Mr. Right Comes Along, breaks yokes and destroys many burdens. It is my desire that this book be used as an instrument to set the captives free and generate meaning and purpose as ladies wait for Mr. Right to come along.

A friend shared with me that his father was a minister fifty years ago. He stated that his dad told him that one day men will become so scarce that women will walk up to men in awe and amazement. He further stated that women would be moved to touch men and squeeze or embrace them because they would not have had an opportunity to be in a man's presence in a long period of time and because men will be in a scarcity.

Many women today are struggling with the lack of a "good man" in their lives. They are frustrated with toxic relationships. Too many women have not witnessed the influence of a positive relationship with a man. Some women talk about their frustration with not being able to find a suitable companion. Some indicate they are puzzled because they cannot keep this man in their life; he will not stay. In essence, she is stressed because she cannot get what she wants. She feels alone and incomplete.

Daddy is often absent or presents a negative image in many ladies' lives. The man who should demonstrate how a man is to love a woman demonstrates a negative image in their lives. Therefore, many women feel they are born with a negative advantage. Too many women are not able to see an example of how a man should treat a lady. They have not witnessed a father demonstrate an example of correction, protection, provision or direction in their life.

The impact of the male/female experience has major effects in many ladies' and men's lives, resulting in depression, anxiety and sometimes explosive behaviors. I witness many individuals having difficulties taking charge of their emotions resulting from sin, guilt, pride, bag of dreams, shame and stress. What I see daily are angry, hurt, stressed and physical and mentally unhealthy women trying to be alright.

I see daily anger not dealt with manifests in negative ways: unpleasant memories, unresolved conflict, unrealistic expectations, un-confessed sin, unexpected financial pressure and uncertain future. Women are restless about Mr. Right and very ambivalent as to whether she will ever enjoy a healthy male/female relationship. Anger not properly dealt with can lead to destruction.

Be ye angry, and sin not; let not the sun go down upon your wrath: Neither give place to the devil. Ephesians 4: 26-26

Most young and mature women desire a healthy relationship with the opposite sex. It is normal and God created us female and male as opposite destined to be attracted to each other. Too many women do not recognize those ingredients which are needed for a healthy relationship. Many women have gotten discouraged feeling broken, busted and disgusted. Many are disappointed and feel they have fallen and they cannot get up. It is normal for man and woman to desire each other.

And the lord said, it is not good that man shall be alone; I will make him a help meet. Genesis: 2:18.

Woman was created from man for man. Woman was not taken from man's head for him to control a woman. Woman was not taken from a man's spine for woman to walk behind a man. Woman was not taken from a man's foot for man to walk or step on woman. She was taken from man's rib close to his heart- for man to love, guide, direct, protect and provide for a woman. She is to walk by his side as his help meet- assisting him in reaching his God -given purpose.

Every man or woman should have a purpose, a goal and yes a plan. If a man does not have a purpose in life the question is: As a man help meet, what will you (woman) help him to reach? Man and woman should seek to know his or her purpose.

We live in a real world and not an ideal world. In the real world, life will sometime unfold in ways that we do not desire. Too many women today are faced with the reality that there is not a significant man in their lives. Women often time find themselves in situations where women "outnumbered" men- not enough available men. Too many men are in prison, on drugs, unemployed, or gay. I am not judging just stating the reality.

And ye shall know the truth, and the truth shall set you free. John 8:32

The Bible states that: **Marriage is honorable in all, and the bed undefiled: whoremongers and adulterers God will judge. Hebrews 13: 4.**

Daily repeat: **I can do all things through Christ who strengthens me. Philippians 4:13.**

"You can be alright until Mr. Right comes along." Let's see what God can do when your natural connects with God's supernatural. THE BEST IS YET TO COME! ENJOY!

The Master's Plan

IN THE BEGINNING

In the beginning, God created the heaven and earth. Just imagine the earth being formless and empty and filled with darkness. Our God, the Creator, spoke light into existence and said: "Let there be light", and there was light. God saw the light was good. God separated the light from the darkness. He called the light "day" and the darkness He called "night."

Before you start placing labels, we sometimes need to put life into proper perspective. On day two, God created the sky and the ocean; on the third day God created the dry land; on the fourth day God created the sun, moon and stars; on the fifth day, God created the birds and the fish and on the sixth day God created animals and man.

"You are so very special!" God said, "Let's make man in my image, in our likeness and let them rule over the fish of the sea, and the birds of the air, over the livestock, over all the earth and over all the creatures that move along the grounds." He gave man dominion over the earth. Pay close attention; God did not give man and woman control over each other.

God created man in his own image, in the image of God He created him; male and female He created. God blessed male and female and told them to be fruitful and increase in number; fill the earth and subdue it.

Just think about this, even though God created us from dust, this is no reason for us to treat another person like dirt. God saw all that He had made and it was very good. Respect is due in our male- female relationships.

Adam had no suitable helper and was alone. So God caused the man to fall in a deep sleep and while he was sleep, He took out the man's rib and created woman and He brought her to man. Please note God did not take a bone from man's skull for man to control a woman. He did not take a woman from man's spine for a woman to walk behind a man. He did not take woman from the bones in a man's foot for his to walk on her.

God took woman from the man's rib, close to man's heart for man to love his special lady like he loves himself- to love her like Christ loved the church. When God brought the woman to the man, he said, "This is bone of my bones and flesh of my flesh; she shall be called woman," for she was taken out of man. God created woman from man for man.

On the seventh day, God rested. Yes, God rested. We need to take the seventh day, the Sabbath Day, and rest. We can rest in the arms of God, casting our cares upon Him because he cares for you. Now the million dollar question is how can Ms. Right be alright until Mr. Right comes along?

We serve a mighty God. Nothing is impossible with God. You do not have to settle with less than God is willing to bless you with. Be willing to be with you until the right one comes along. If you do not want to be with you, why would anyone else want to be with you? Continue to read and find peace in knowing you can be alright until Mr. Right comes along.

DOES GOD HAVE A PLAN FOR ME?

Waiting sometimes can be frustrating. You may ask many questions like: Am I okay? Am I beautiful? Will true love ever come my way? Did God forget about me? When will Mr. Right come- at age twenty or forty?

While you wait for Mr. Right, a wonderful place to be is to reflect on God's plan for your life. Regardless to what it looks like, regardless of the circumstances, God still has a plan and purpose for your life. I assure you God has not forgotten about you. Just be aware that sometimes God calms the storm but more often He lets the storm calms you.

God loves you and is never going to give up on you. He created you and will never leave you or forsake you. Therefore, sit back and know that you are in good hands as you wait on Mr. Right. God has a plan and purpose for you. Before He formed you in your mother's womb, He predestined you with His Divine purpose.

For I know the thoughts that I think toward you, saith the Lord, thoughts of peace, and not of evil, to give you an expected end. Jeremiah 29:11.

God knows the plan he has for you. God knows exactly where you are in your present growth and development. He knows exactly what level you are at this present hour. He understands all the issues, struggles, problems and drama that you are dealing with. God may not like where your life is right now but rest in the assurance He is not going to leave you.

Every issue, problem or situation you are currently dealing with is not about your past or present existence. It is about your future. The enemy's or devil's goal is to abort the destiny God has on your life. So hold on to God's unchanging hands no matter what it looks like. God is always with you-carrying you, loving you and working it all for your good.

Please do not curse your pain. Do not curse scars. You are encouraged to forget those things behind you. You are to keep reaching for the things before you. You should daily press toward the "prize" of the higher calling. Your efforts will not be in vain. God is calling you to great vision, great expectations, and to a great destiny.

How much do you trust God? Do you trust God with your life regardless of what you see? Is there a shadow of doubt because you are single and alone? One ounce of doubt can change the way we view God's presence in our lives.

Can God take your heartache, your trials, your suffering and your sin and turn them into something good? The answer is yes He can. Is there anything too difficult for God to do? No.

God had a divine plan for Abraham and Sarah. Sarah was beyond child bearing age. She was ninety years old.

Then Abraham fell upon his face, and laughed, and said in his heart, Shall a child be born unto him that is a hundred years old? And shall Sarah that is ninety years old bear? Genesis 17:16.

When Sarah heard God repeat His promise of a son to her husband, she laughed and the Lord asked Abraham, "Why did Sarah laugh, saying, Shall I indeed bear a child, when I am so old?" Have you ever doubted God's ability to supply your needs? Have you doubted God sending Mr. Right in your life? Never give up on God.

Like Sarah, we get tired of waiting and forget what it feels like to wait and live in the goodness of God's will. Instead of waiting, we want to rush ahead and go in another direction to get immediate gratification. We later suffer as a result of our decision.

Timing is everything to God. God has a set time for the events to unfold in our lives. He has a set time for Mr. Right to appear in your life. Visiting a fortune teller or fasting according to your own desires will not change God's mind. God's timing is motivated by heaven's timetable and not our timetable. We miss a blessing when we think we can convince God to move more quickly or change His mind.

I encourage you to wait on God's perfect timing. Let's not take short cuts around God's plan for our life. Sarah not only laughed at God's plan (for her and husband, Abraham, to give birth at an old age), but Sarah doubted God's promise. Sarah had taken matters into her own hands. The Middle East remains in conflict today because of this decision. Sarah was convinced that God was not going to allow her to have a son. What did she do? She recruited her maid to have a child with her husband. Ishmael's birth set off a "tidal wave" that is still moving today.

Let us not allow doubt to cripple us. Let's not let doubt cause us to experience a "fallen" future. If you are tempted to doubt God's love for you and you feel Mr. Right does not exist and you will always be alone, stop and ask Him to speak to your heart and encourage you to wait.

I hope you receive added assurance in knowing that God loves you. Regardless to your circumstances or whatever issues you are dealing with in your life, God still loves you. God loves you if you are single or married. God loves you if you have been hurt, broken, or busted. God loves you if a man rejected you and left you for another woman. God loves you if you are lonely and alone.

You may ask why I quote scriptures. **I do so because God is the one who has all the answers you need, and each answer is found in His Word.** You may not know exactly where you are going. Believe me when you get where He has called you to go, you will experience a miraculous blessing.

Instead of thinking, What about me and my desires, the right questions to ask are "Lord, what is your desire for my life? God, what is your will for me? God, please show me your plan, and make it clear so I can do your will. God, is it your will that I be single at this time in my life? God, what is your will for me and Mr. Right? Be patient and wait on the Lord. You can be alright until Mr. Right comes along.

THE MORAL COMPASS

As the world turns, we can now meet people all over the world via travel and technology. The world is made of all types of people-young and old, different ages, male and female, and different ethnic groups. Just think what the world would be like if we were all the same- looked the same and acted the same? What a boring world this would be.

God created each one of us differently. We have different identities with different finger prints. We possess our individual DNA. Believe it- God did not make any mistakes when He created you uniquely as you are.

Just think because you are different, you will make different choices and decisions. There are people in this world who are moved by positive and negative forces. Just think you have the power to choose who you will allow to be a significant part of our life. The power is definitely in the choice.

You actually started on a quest of life the day you were born. It may have been years before it became apparent that you were constantly searching. You could have been searching for something you never had. Sometimes, you tried to forget about it. Your search could have been more important than anything in life. Sometimes, you may have tried to lose yourself in other things so there could be only time to reflect on the important issue of the moment.

At the loneliest moments in your life, you may have looked at women and men and wondered if they were seeking something they could not describe but knew what they wanted and needed. But you are not alone. All mankind is traveling with you; for, all mankind is on the same quest. All humanity is seeking the answer to the moral sickness, confusion and the spiritual emptiness that oppress the world. All mankind is crying out for guidance, for comfort, and for peace. Some think that they will be happy if they could just meet Mr. Right.

Let us therefore come boldly unto the throne of grace, that we may obtain mercy, and find grace in time of need. Hebrews 4:16.

Morals can be defined as expressing or teaching a conception of right behavior sanctioned by or operative on one's conscience or technical judgment. The question is should we compromise our morals? Should we compromise our morals in the name of love, for the sake of our male/female relationship, our man, our beau, or our lover?

I want to bless you with this truth: Never compromise your morals, principles, character and definitely never compromise your belief in God. Believe me no man is worth this sacrifice-no matter how handsome he is; no matter how much money he has; no matter if he is a famous football player or actor. As a matter of fact, obedience is better than sacrifice. Not to frighten you but to share with you the truth- if you are not obedient, you will sacrifice something- peace, happiness, joy and yes, sometimes, you may sacrifice your life.

Life on earth becomes worth living when we establish a personal and intimate relationship with God. Through this relationship we grow in faith. Our faith in God gives us the courage which equips us with the mental or moral strength to risks opposition. Our courage generates liberty which gives us freedom to move around and make moral choices. In order to stand for something, you have to stand against something.

We are human flesh on a spiritual journey. The spirit is the energy, drive, force, motivation and power which move us to do what we do in life. The spirit serves to ignite the human state of being. Our destiny in life is determined by our personal choices to be governed by the power of God or by a lower power-the devil. There is an intrinsic force that can resist and overcome all outward pressure. Our relationship with God can provide strength to enable us to overcome evil or destruction.

Our ethics, morals and principles are governed by our choices. Based on our choices, our character (moral excellence) is built. You have the liberty to choose what is positive or negative. Our choice to use knowledge for good or evil determines our abundance and prosperity: Mr. Right, good family, husband, children, or job.

Woman has the personal power to choose the man in her life and not wait on the man to choose her-power of choice. Therefore, you have the personal power to allow yourself to experience life and make choices even in relationships. Interestingly, there are so many men to choose from- men with positive and negative character.

The reality is women often have to weed through the negative to get to the men with positive character. This means you will have to face reality and understand there are still some good men out there in the world but you must allow yourself to gain the proper information to make the right choices with direction from God. You have to know who and what are good for you. You may have to let go of some men in your life for God to send the man He wills for you and your life enhancement.

Do not get discouraged when a certain man does not meet your package of qualities you would like to see in your man-Mr. Right. Do not be disappointed, depressed or anxious. Allow this to be an opportunity for you see that God did not allow you to connect to this man, no matter what you think you want. God is blessing you and instructing you that this man is not Mr. Right but Mr. Wrong, and this too is a blessing. Whatever is not God sent- can be used by God. Wait to see what God is going to do. Live with expectations!

As I have stated, please do not compromise your morals, principles, character and most of all your belief in God. These are the important virtues which can be used to guide and direct you in your decisions. When it comes to connecting to Mr. Right, it is absolutely crucial that God and the moral compass guide you in making your decisions. Remember in your relationship(s) with the opposite sex, it is very important to seek first the kingdom of God and His righteousness and all those other things will be added.

Sisters, just because a man does not have money, stuff or material things do not mean that he is not worthy. Good men sometimes fall on hard times especially when the economy is depressed. You sometimes need to overlook the circumstance and see his heart, love, honesty, loyalty and yes respect.

You cannot make a man be who you want him to be, but you can surely encourage him and contribute to molding him into a winner and maybe witness him becoming the next Governor or President.

Inspect the package. Look at the fringe benefits or blessings. Take time to look at the gift inside and out. Everything that looks good may not be good. Do not judge a book by looking at the cover. Everything good to you might not be good for you. Every person who appears to be good to you may not be your friend. The devil sometimes gives gifts, too. The package may not be wrapped attractively but inside the package you may find silver, gold or diamonds.

Let God be your moral compass to direct your life. Seek God's direction on which way you should go-north, south, east or west. Ask God if you are making correct decision(s). Be careful who you listen to in determining if this one is Mr. Right. I made a mistake by allowing my flesh to instruct me on Mr. Right. I paid for this decision dearly. I was infatuated with the bedroom eyes. I encourage you not to lean to your own understanding but in all that you do acknowledge God and He will direct your path. "You can be alright until Mr. Right comes along."

Trust in the Lord with all thine heart; and lean not unto thine own understanding. In all thy ways acknowledge him, and he shall direct thy paths. Proverbs 3: 5-6.

TRANFORMATION OF YOUR MIND

It is easy to get caught up in romantic dreams. You might even have visions of your wedding day and beyond. However, while these thoughts may be enjoyable, they are illusions. They may produce overwhelming desires that you have no means of satisfying.

Hope deferred makes the heart sick. Proverbs 13:12

Daydreams can distort your judgment. The shrewd one considers his steps. This means using common sense and sound judgment. How can you be shrewd in being alright until Mr. Right comes along?

The simple believeth every word; but the prudent man looketh well to his going. Proverbs 14:15

Wherever the mind goes, the body will follow. As the United Negro College Funds slogan says: "A mind is a terrible thing to waste." The way a woman thinks will affect her feelings. The way a woman feels will affect her decisions. A woman's decision will affect her actions. A woman's actions can become habit forming. A woman's habits will affect her character. A woman's character will ultimately affect her destiny.

Ms. Right should have the right frame of mind when she focuses on her relationship with a man. Some women may feel that there are no good men left in the world for them. Some women may feel "all men are dogs." Some women may feel all the good men are married. Some women may feel they will never get married. Some women may even wonder is it God's plan that they are not married. I have heard several women say I have never gone on a "real" date with a man. Some women ask do I need to lower my standards to find Mr. Right. Let's ask God for a transformation of our mind.

Hold on! You do not have to fear. Fear is **f**ear-**e**vidence-**a**ppearing-**r**eal. Fear knocked on the door; faith opened the door and there was nothing there. You do not have to fear that Mr. Right will never come along. You do not need to waste your time concentrating on the notion you will never get married. In the faith realm, you have to see it to see it.

I beseech you therefore, brethren, by the mercies of God that you present your bodies as a living sacrifice, holy and acceptable unto God, which is your reasonable service. And be not conformed to this world; but be ye transformed by the renewing of the mind, that ye may prove what is good and acceptable, and perfect, will of God. Romans 12: 1-2.

Sisters, please do not conform to the world's way of thinking. The renewing of the mind means that we are to replace our thoughts with God's thoughts. Sisters, let us focus on God's promises. Let's not "box" God in. There is a man out there "looking for his ribs." He is looking for you. You do not have to find him. He is capable and will find you. Believe me every man in his right mind is searching for Ms. Right. If he is not in his right mind, he is Mr. Wrong and you do not want him because he is not sent to you by God. If he is not sent to you by God, whom is he sent by and what are his motives?

You may ask: How does renewing of the mind pertain to my particular situation? I am the one who is lonely. You may say I desire to have a companion in my life to share life daily experiences. You may say I go to bed each night with no one to hold me close.

I get it! I do understand where you are coming from. We still have to keep the faith- Now faith is the substance of things hoped for; the evidence of things unseen. We have to be conscience of what is the will of God. We have to renew our minds through the application of the Word of God. This is done by the reading, studying, speaking and applying the Word of God in our daily life. We need to have the now kind of faith.

For God has not given us the spirit of fear; but one of power, of love, and a sound mind. 2 Timothy 1:7.

You are encouraged to read the Word of God in the Bible (Basic–Instructions-Before- Leaving- Earth) and apply the Word of God as it applies to your situation especially as it relates to Mr. Right.

For the word of God is quick, and powerful, and sharper than a two-edged sword piercing to the even dividing asunder of soul and spirit, and the joints and marrow, and is a discerner of the thoughts and intents of the heart. Hebrews 4:12

Renewing your mind has to be done on a daily basis. The mind is constantly functioning with different thoughts-some negative and positive. The Word of God is effective in replacing thoughts derived from thinking like the world. Reading and applying the Bible will illuminate your mind with the truth which is contrary to the way the world thinks.

Renew your mind with positive thoughts: God is preparing my husband for me. When it is God's timing, Mr. Right will come along. Until that time we have to know that all things are working together for the good of those who love God and are called according to His plan or purpose.

Remember God's timing is not your timing, and His ways are not our ways. Therefore some male/female experiences we perceive as negative, God is working those experiences for our good. This truth will be revealed as time progresses. We may be disappointed that the relationship did not work out, but this could be a blessing in disguise.

God answers prayers in His perfect timing. If the timing is not right God says no; if you are not right God says grow; and when everything is right God says go. Submission to God's will manifests that whatever God does is done for our best. A no answer could be God's way of protecting us. An answer of grow allows us to get prepared for our blessing. Go is the green light which reveals that the timing is right, and individually you are ready to receive God's blessing. Sometimes, blessing received too early can be harmful to you especially if you are not prepared to deal with the responsibilities.

We will have mountain and valley experiences in our lives. Anything that is not God sent can be God used. God will not put any more on us than we can bear. Remember all that is good and perfect comes from God. I know many of my sisters have experienced much pain resulting from not having the right man in their life-Mr. Right.

Just be assured God can take lemons and make lemonade; God can take bricks and make stepping stones; God can take scars and turn into stars; God can take the test and make the testimony; God can take the mess and make the message; God can take pain and make passion; and God can take misery and make the ministry. The master mess can become the master piece. It sounds like a miracle to me. Only God can work miracles.

Replace negative ungodly thought with the word of God. Believe me if you will practice thinking and focusing on the words of God, you will experience change in your life. There is awesome power in the word of God.

The important thing is not to let our experience make us bitter but better. No matter how it looks, God can take the negative experience and make it work for your good. Hold on Mr. Right can come along. If Mr. Right is delayed or does not come when we want him to, we can dedicate our time, energy and spirit in doing something worthwhile for the glory of God and the good of His people. Remember a vision delayed is not a vision denied. God may not come when you want Him to, but He is always on time. You can be alright until Mr. Right comes along.

Saved and Single

HAVE AN ATTITUDE OF GRATITUDE AND THANKSGIVING

How happy are you right now? Do you even know? Most women know what make their parents and their man happy. However, when it comes to awareness about the little, specific things in life that brings them joy and peace, they often come up short.

A man born of a woman or a woman born of a woman will have a few days and lots of trouble according to the word of God. We will sometime experience pain, hurt, disappointment and defeat. Yet it is so important to move away from negativity (the natural) and move to the positive realm of life (the spiritual).

You are encouraged to be thankful to God even when you are going through. The secret to life is to learn to make the most out of whatever life presents to you. Develop an attitude of gratitude and thanksgiving-even if you are single, even if you are not involved in a relationship with Mr. Right.

God is a spirit; and they that worship him must worship him in spirit and in truth. John 4:24

No one enjoys the pain which comes with hurt we experience in life. Yet hurt comes to instruct us. I know you hurt when the love of your life left you for another woman. I know you hurt due to the reality he cheated on you. I know you hurt when he married your best friend. I feel your pain when the love of your life got another lady pregnant. You are still encouraged to praise God even when it hurts. Find something to thank God for. Go beyond your breaking point-pain and disappointment.

God will see you through. Regardless of the circumstances, praise God anyway with an attitude of gratitude and thanksgiving. Attitude is an outward expression of inner feelings. Your attitude is disposition and how you carry yourself. Your attitude will ultimately determine your altitude and how high you will climb in life.

Believe me I know because God saw me through the storm when I was hurt by the man I loved. My pain became someone else gain and also became my passion in founding United Families of America, Inc. I encourage you to sing hallelujah anyhow. Praising God completes your faith. Praising God unlocks doors which have been locked in your life. When praises go up the blessings of God come down.

Do you praise your way out of trouble? God deserves your praises privately and publicly. God deserve your praises in the storm, rain and when you see the rainbow. The amount of time you praise God indicates your relationship with God. In time of conflict and challenges, we have to learn to praise God the most.

Learn to praise God when it is not convenient and when it does not feel good. Praise God when you feel hurt, broken, busted and disgusted. Praise God when you are in pain and you feel you do not have a friend in this world. Praise God when you are alone and you do not feel you are loved. Praise the Lord while you are waiting on Mr. Right.

Even if Mr. Right does not come along when you want him to, praise God anyway. You can still find something to be thankful for. You can still be about your Father God's business. This is the time to ask God what is in this situation for you. This is the time to ask God to help you become better and not bitter. This is the time to illustrate that more than anything, you want to be in the Divine will of God- not my will but your will, Lord. This is time to demonstrate WOTL- waiting on the Lord. Wait on the Lord to renew your strength.

Even though tears may be flowing down your eyes because the man of your life has decided he no longer wants to date you, find something to thank God for. This drives the devil crazy. The test of greatness is to survive frustration. Learn to get the treasure out of the trial.

I have had conversation with many women who complain that they do not have a man in their life. I have participated in discussion with many who speak of the abuse they have received from men who they thought loved them. Some talk about how they were used by the men they trusted. Be thankful you did not continue to exist in this toxic relationship. Yes, sisters, have the attitude of gratitude and thanksgiving that God lifted you out of this mess. Thank God for His grace and mercy.

As ye have therefore received Jesus Christ the Lord, so walk ye in Him: Rooted and built up in, and established in faith, as ye have been taught, abounding therein with thanksgiving. Colossians 2:6-7.

Stop cheating God by treating Him like He is your "sugar daddy" and start worshipping and praising him. Give God thanks in all things, in all situations and circumstances because He is truly worthy to be praised.

When thou pass through the waters, I will be with thee; and through the rivers, they shall not overflow thee, when thou walkest through the fire, thou shall not be burned; neither shall the flame kindle upon thee. Isaiah 43:2

I know in dealing with life's male/female relationship, it presents many challenges. You are naturally attracted to men but the result for many women is tremendous pain, disappointment, shame and regrets. Just know that through it all you are more than a conqueror. The "master mess" can become the "Masterpiece."

Is there anything too hard for God? While you are waiting on God to send Mr. Right to find you, ask God to work on you while you are alone. Ask God to make you complete while you are alone. Ask the Potter to mold you into the person He wants you to be.

Time alone can be a special gift from God. Do not focus on your insecurities about self because you are alone. Do not allow external pressures of society, family or friends to move you to experience negative emotions.

You can increase your faith through thanksgiving. Believe it because it has been done. Your husband- Mr. Right- is on his way. Praise God with the right attitude-the attitude of gratitude and thanksgiving. Who will you serve this day? "You can be alright until Mr. Right comes along."

THE POWER OF THE SPOKEN WORDS

I am sure you have heard the saying "Sticks and stones may break your bones but words will never hurt you." Wrong! Wrong! Words can and do hurt. There is life and death in the tongue. Words can build and destroy.

Be mindful of the words that you speak to yourself and others. It is often necessary to "weed" our minds of negative thinking. Imagine that you plant a vegetable garden this spring. Let's say you plant collard greens, okra, corn, and tomatoes. A few weeks after planting, the weeds began to grow around the garden plants. If you do not weed the garden, what happens to the garden? The weeds will choke the garden plants and the plants will die. You must pull the weeds up. You have to weed your life of the negatives thoughts and emotions resulting from the past. Do not let your past cripple your future.

Every time we open our mouth, men look into our mind. We have to "weed" our minds of negative thinking and replace those words with positive words or affirmations. For example: There are no good men in America. Replace these words with. I do not know all men. I am sure there are some good men in America or somewhere in the world.

There is power in the spoken word. What is on the inside of you will manifest itself on the outside. Guard your heart and renew your mind. Your soul (mind, will and emotions) is affected by the words that you speak.

The tongue is a fire, a world of iniquity: so is the tongue among our members; that it defileth the whole body; and setteth on fire the course of nature; and it set on fire of hell. James 3:6.

I know you may say that I continue to focus on the issue of attracting Mr. Right from a spiritual prospective. You may say I am privileged and do not understand. You may say you do not get it! Believe me I do get it. I have been in toxic relationship(s). I have been hurt and used. I have been there and I have seen that. I too fall short of the glory of God. I have grown to know that God is the truth, the way and the life. Through God all things are possible. God can empower us to be alright until Mr. Right comes along. It is recommended for you to trust God all the way.—not part of the way or when it is convenient for you.

The Word is as powerful as a two edged sword. We will continue to give God the praises for all things. We will give God praises if we are single or married. We will give God the glory even though we have been hurt by a toxic relationship. We will give God the praises if a "game" has been played on us. We will praise God if we were left after a divorce with three children to raise and nurture alone. We will give God the glory when He delivers us out of a domestic violence situation. When the praises go up, the blessings come down.

Speak words of love! Speak words of power! Speak words of life! Speak the following words in your relationships: I Love You! I just called because I wanted to hear your voice. Is there anything I can do to bless you today? I miss you so much when I am away from you! I am so sorry I hurt you! You did a fantastic job! I need to embrace you in my life! I am proud of you! Will you be a blessing to me by going out with me tonight? I do not care what the world says. I know I could not have done this without you! You were right and I was wrong. Thank you for being the man of God that you are!

We have to be conscious of what words we speak. We do not have to worry about finding Mr. Right. We should avoid negative thinking and negative speaking: "All men cheat." "There are no good men out there." "All the men I come in contact with are raggedy-behind lazy men who do not want to work and want me to take care of them." These statements are generalizations because you do not know all men and have not met all men.

It will not be sunny every day in our lives. We will sometimes see rain, storms and tornadoes. Satan will create doubt encouraging you to think negative and to experience fear. You have the power to move to a positive place. You can do all things through Christ who strengthens you. If your mind can conceive it, you can believe it and you can achieve it.

Do not let anyone tell you that your wings are broken and you cannot fly. If you can look up, you can get up. Every day you get up tell the devil "This is the day that the Lord has made and I am going to rejoice and be glad in it." When you glorify God, Satan is horrified. Whatever God brings you to, He will bring you through.

You cannot be pitiful and powerful at the same time. Complaining allows us to stay in the valley longer. Complain and remain; praise and be raised. We all will go through mountain and valley experience at some point in our lives. Even when we are going through the valley, we should remember you cannot get to the mountain top unless you go through the valley. It is in the valley where growth takes place.

I believe there is power in words. You are encouraged to speak positive affirmations to yourself daily: I love the highest and best in people. I now draw myself the highest and best in people. I give thanks for ever-increasing health, beauty, and prosperity. I give thanks that every day I am growing stronger and stronger. Divine intelligence now shows me everything I know. I speak peace, joy and prosperity in my life. "I can be alright until Mr. Right comes along."

PRAYER CHANGES THINGS: ASK GOD FOR MR. RIGHT

So you are alone? What are you praying for? God can give you the desires of your heart. No prayer-no power. Little prayer- little power. Much prayer-much power. So let us have a little talk with Jesus and tell Him about our troubles. We do not have to tweet Him or Facebook Him. His telephone line is never busy. God knows our heart and He knows our heart desires. God knows all things.

Therefore, we can be totally honest with God. We can share our secrets with God. Just as we peel the onion of life back one layer at a time, even in tears-we can do likewise with God.

Life is about 10% of what happens to you and 90% about what you do about what happens to you. Sometimes we spend too much time talking about our situation. Too often we spend enormous time speaking and gossiping on our telephone, telling our friends about the drama in our life and our relationships.

How about spending time with Jesus telling him about our situation? Speak to the mountain. So you have been used and abused. You feel broke, busted and disgusted. Tell God about it. Speak to your loneliness, speak to your brokenness, speak to your heartache, speak to your depression, and speak to your anxiety.

Jesus answered and said unto them. Verily I say unto you, if ye have faith, and doubt not, ye shall not only do this which is done to the fig tree, but also if ye shall say unto the mountain, be thou removed, and be thou cast into the sea; it shall be done. And all things, whatsoever ye shall ask in prayer, believing, ye shall receive. Matthew 21: 21-22

No matter how it looks God wants to bless you. He loves you and me so much that He gave His only Son Jesus Christ so that we can be redeemed and reconciled back to Him. Sometimes, my mind becomes so consumed with the fact that Jesus loves me so much that He actually died on the cross for my sins. Have you ever known anyone who loves you the way God and Jesus love you? All I can say is wow! What a God we serve! When I try to describe God, He is so awesome- I am move to describe Him as un-describable.

Prayer is another way of spending personal and intimate time with God. When we pray, we can strengthen our relationship with God. Yes, it is great to focus on religion and going to church but please focus on your personal relationship with God. Prayer is vital means to strengthening your relationship with God and His son, Jesus Christ.

When I pray I like to focus on the acronyms: ACTS. The A in ACTS reminds me to pray for Adoration of God and His son Jesus Christ. The C in ACTS reminds me to pray for the Confession of my sins. The T in ACTS motivates me to give God the glory for many Thanksgivings God is bestowing in my life. The S in ACTS moves me to pray for the Supplication of my needs and desires.

When we pray, let's not limit God because God can do exceedingly and abundantly more than anything we can dream or imagine. So what are you praying for at this time and season in your life? Because we serve a mighty God, we can order Mr. Right. We can ask God to send Mr. Right who can be signed, sealed and delivered by God. Not someone we will just settle with to have a man in our life-but a man who is led by God.

My questions to you are: "If the man you desire in your life is not led by God, can he lead you? Do you want a man in your life who will love you like he loves himself? Does this man love himself? Do you want a man in your life who would love you as Christ loves the church? Does this man know Christ and does he go to church? Can he guide, direct, protect and provide for you? Can he lead and are you willing to submit to him? Can he relate to you spiritual, physical, mentally, emotional and socially. Can he provide for you and the family? Does he want to work? What are his short and long range goals? What are his views on relationships? Where does he see the outcome of his relationship with you?

Can this man enhance your life and you enhance his life? This is a very important question. Many women are praying for God to send Mr. Right. Are you Ms. Right? Many women want the man to be their savior. Christ is the only Savior. Prayer creates a path where there is none and turns your stumbling blocks into building blocks. "You can be alright until Mr. Right to come along."

SAVED AND SINGLE

- Author Unknown -
What makes you think that just because I am
An attractive woman of Godly intelligence
That I am incomplete without a mate?
Who told you that without a man?
Something's missing from my life?
And if so what would that be?
Love?
I love myself
And more importantly
I love the Lord.
He told me when I delight in Him,
He will give me the desires of my heart
Security?
I have everything I need according to His riches in glory.
Intimacy?
Now, how's a man going to get to know me?
When he doesn't even know who he is in the Lord
See my Father told me I'm above a ruby's worth
And a gem does not seek
It is sought I'm single and that's all right with me
See, it's not that I detest co-dependency
As a woman I know it is not my role
To chase after any man
Esther 2:14 reads
That I am to wait on my king and when he's delighted in me He will call

Me by my name.
My Lord does not intend for me to be needy or desperate.
It is not my job to convince him
Or Convict him of that,
My mate will already know it
And consistently show it
And he will stay on his knees daily.

When I pray, you answer me, and encourage me by giving me the strength I need. Psalms 138:3

Call unto me, and I will answer thee, and shew thee great and mighty things, which thou knowest not. Jeremiah 33:3.

Ask, and it shall be given you; seek and ye shall find; knock, and it shall be opened unto you. Matthew 7:7

PRAYER FOR A COMPANION

Our Father......
Eternal Father of the Universe, the Creator of all that is good
Whose presence I feel within me each and every day, please
Help me to attract a loving, understanding, supportive and deserving companion.
Father God, please send the man I desire to make my life complete on this earth-
Either as a friend, mate or husband.
Father God, you are the only omnipotent one. You are the only omnipresent one.
God you know I possess a sincere and unselfish interest in others.
If it is your will, Father God, help me to know that there is a Mr. Right seeking me
As earnestly as I am waiting for that someone.
Help me to have the "now" kind of faith that the love and companionship
For which I desire and yearn, is within my reach.
Help me, Dear Father, to put aside my feelings of loneliness
And to look forward, with faith and expectation to those things hoped for,
To the making of new friends and associates until Mr. Right comes along.
Help me, Father God, to remember that I must be a friend to have a friend.
Help me to know that I must love to beget love.
From this moment, I promise to allow You God to do a work in me.
God I ask you to give me a new heart and the right spirit.
I will open my mind and heart and send out my call
For that someone I need- to be all that I need him to be.
God, please grant me patience to wait until you send Mr. Right in my life.
Lord, it would be a blessing to embrace someone who will guide, direct, protect
And provide for me. God grant me the ability to submit to first God and second to
The husband God has prepared for me.
I am opened to a man who will love me as he loves himself and as Christ loves the

Church. I do ask this in faith that this prayer has been heard
And is even now answered in Jesus' Name
And I thank you, Father God, for the evidence and manifestation of your unfailing love. Father God, please keep me-now and forever more as I wait for Mr. Right to be sent to me by you.
Amen!

Therefore I say unto you, What things so ever ye desire, when ye pray, believe that ye receive them, and ye shall have them. Mark 11:24.

Have faith and believe your prayers are working. Be still for a moment and think about what you have prayed for recently. Was it for some material item or was it for something you really needed, like patience, wisdom, peace of mind, compassion or companionship? The next time a woman crosses your path and you find yourself coveting her man, remember God has created a man specifically for you. All your gifts have your name written on them. "You can be alright until Mr. Right comes along."

But if we hope for what we do not have, we wait for it patiently. In the same way, the Spirit helps us in our weakness. We do not know what we ought to pray for; but the Spirit itself intercedes for us with groans that words cannot express. And he who searches our hearts knows the mind of the Spirit, because the Spirit intercedes for the saints in accordance with God's will. Romans 8:25-27 NIV

I do not know how hip this sounds. Nevertheless, it is important to pray about all things. I believe praying for God to send Mr. Right in your life is truly in Divine Order. Just think about how our relationships would be impacted if we allow God to direct our path. Yet, too many of us are guilty of being attracted to a mate or significant other based on what our flesh dictates.

Wait on the Lord! He may not come when we want him to but God is always on time. God's timing is not our timing and His ways are not our ways. Be patient and have faith that we can be alright until Mr. Right comes along.

SUBMISSION TO GOD IS THE WAY TO GO

Are you going to submit to man, the world or God? Strong emotions often move a woman to try hard to satisfy and please her man. We dress to get his attention. We study what please his every desire. We often deceive ourselves and after two dates we began to try on his last name and marriage is not the reality. We ask ourselves how does Mrs. Jones sound. How does Mrs. Harris sound?

We sometimes make excuses for his bad behavior. Many women are desperate enough to provide for a man's financial desires. We pay his rent, utilities, and the cellphone bill. Many women do all this in the name of LOVE. Yes, it makes me wonder as Tina Turner sings: "What's love got to do with it."

Please note, the woman is submitting to her man and not her husband. How can we submit to a man who has not submitted to God himself?

Submit yourselves therefore to God. Resist the devil and he will flee from you. James 4:7

Be not wise in thine own eyes: fear the Lord and depart from evil. Proverbs 3:7.

Does the man want you to fornicate? Submit to God.

Does the man refuse to get a job but want you to rent him a car? Submit to God.

Does this man want to be your "sugar daddy" and remain with his wife? Submit to God.

Is this man in a relationship with you but his Facebook page shows he is not in a relationship? Submit to God.

Is this man handsome, sales illegal marijuana daily and offer to buy a house for you? Submit to God.

Does this man offer you money for sex? Submit to God.

Does this man abuse women but tells you, you are different? Submit to God.

Does this man tell you that he hates his mom but loves you? Submit to God.

Are you in Christ? Who will you serve this day? When you are in Christ something has to change. Old things pass away and you become a new creature. Things you use to do, you do not do anymore. You recognize you live in this world but you are not of this world. You have decided to submit to God and not man or the world. You are living inspired by God and not by man or the world.

Be very aware when men try to get you to move away from the will of God. Evil likes to prey on weakness. Please do not be side tracked by a man's desire to have dominion and control over your life. It will sometimes look like love. It will sometimes feel like love. Love never fails. Man will fail you. Love keeps on giving while lust is constantly taking from you.

There are some men and women who believe in the" three (3) day rule." After three dates, too many men feel they should get "some." Do I have to define "some"? After three dates, sex should be the prize.

Would you believe I have experience ordained ministers of God try to persuade me that God does not frown on sex outside of marriage? Man often will try to persuade you to submit to him. Get to know God for yourself and be convinced that God's principles are universal and we are to only have faith in God. I say submit to God.

Beware that you do not forget not the Lord thou God…Otherwise, when you build fine houses and settle down and when your herbs and flocks grow large and your silver and gold increase and all you have

is multiplied, then your heart will become proud and you will forget the Lord your God. Deuteronomy 8: 10-14

Interestingly, God does not control you. God is all powerful and allows you your free and permissive will. God allows you the ability to choose: God, the world or man. When someone is controlling you, he or she is practicing witchcraft or voodoo.

In relationships, sometimes the man or woman plays games to try and control each other. Control strategies are used to get the upper hand moving the other individuals to do his or her will. Sisters, please become aware of manipulation, intimidation, guilt trips, threats and bodily harm. These are all control strategies. These are all means to get you to submit to others will- not your will and definitely not the will of God.

Ladies, your body is not Best Western Hotel. Stop letting men come and go as they please. Let God be the Lord of your life. God is pleased when you willingly choose Him. We may have the plan but give God the eraser. Therefore, you are encouraged to submit to God. Remember, it is not over until God says it is over. "You can be alright until Mr. Right comes along."

Therefore, my beloved brethren, be ye steadfast, unmovable, always abounding in the work of the Lord, forasmuch as ye know that your labor is not in vain in the Lord. 1 Corinthians 15:58

Love the One You See in the Mirror

THE POWER OF INFORMATION

There is power in information. Those people with information will control those people without information. I am motivated by the passage in the Bible (Hosea 4:6).

My people are destroyed for lack of knowledge: because thou hast rejected knowledge. I will also reject thee, that thou shalt be no priest to me: seeing thou hast forgotten the law of thy God. I will also forget thy children. Hosea 4:6

As the world turns, it sometimes becomes so easy to experience a confused mind. We often get caught up in so much drama that is not important. We put little emphasis on those things that are most important. Drama drains you of power. We get caught up in the "games of life."

We use our personal power in wrong ways. Personal power is not in anything outside of you. Yet in today's society, our personal power is invested in how to obtain more things. Personal power is not in our cars, companions, drugs, sex, color of skin (ethnicity), clothes you wear, or where you live. Power is within you. The Spirit of God is within you. Do not confuse having less with being less, having more with being more, or what you do with being who you are, or what you have with who you are.

Do you further confuse your mind in thinking you need more things? Too often women desire for Mr. Right to be aligned directly with how they can obtain more material things. Too many women get caught up in what the man can do for me. Spend some time on getting to know the man and ask God is he Mr. Right.

I challenge you to get yourself "some i-n-f-o-r-m-a-t-i-o-n." Information is power but wisdom is supreme. Information equates to knowledge; understanding equates to comprehension; and wisdom equates to application. Learn pertinent substantive information and learn to apply it to your life even while you wait for Mr. Right.

When wisdom entereth into thine heart, and knowledge is pleasant unto thy soul. Discretion shall preserve thee, understanding shall keep thee. To deliver thee from the way of the evil man, from the man that speaketh forward things. Proverbs 2: 10-12.

I often think about the days I attended Pine Park Elementary School. During those times, it was fashionable to take enriched bread to school. It could have been Sunbeam or Colonial bread. The point is there were some of us whose parents could not afford to give us enriched bread to take to school for lunch. So the question is: What did we do? We took what our parents could afford for us to take for lunch. Guess what type of bread we took to school? Our parents took biscuits split them open and filled them with sausage, eggs, peanut butter or whatever they could afford, and wrapped them in waxed paper. We did not have aluminum foil or saran wrap. Thank God they did not use newspaper.

Guess what? There were many of us who would put the biscuits under our table and pinch off the biscuits trying to conceal that we did not have any enriched bread. One day a young man told me (about the biscuit), "I was ashamed and I ate the bad boy before I got to school."

Just think if we had received the correct information, we would have move from a confused mind to a mind filled with business savvy. I could be a wealthy woman today because I would be marketing and selling my mommy's biscuits. Just think about this: everywhere you go today, restaurant chains are selling biscuits- Kentucky Fried Chicken, McDonald, Hardees and more. Popeye's Chicken makes a biscuits that tastes just like my mommy's biscuit. I did not have the correct i-n-f-o-r-m-a-t-i-o-n.

Correct information can determine whether you see the glass of your life as half empty or half filled. You can weed your mind of negative thinking. You can move your body from negative thinking and behavior as you wait for Mr. Right to come along. It behooves us to slow the process down and allow ourselves time to get to know who we are first and also get to know the person we are attracted to.

While you are waiting on Mr. Right, it is extremely important to get information to enable you to make sound decisions. Stop saying "I can't" and replace that thought with "I can." Life is not a destination but a journey. Enjoy your journey as you wait for Mr. Right to come along.

Finally, brethren, whatsoever things are true, whatsoever things are honest, whatsoever are just, whatsoever things are pure, whatsoever things are lovely, whatsoever things are of good report; if there be any virtue, and if there be any praise, think on these things. Philippians 4:8

There are too many people today who are caught up in the battle of the mind. I am convinced that there are three (3) types of people who inhabit this world. (1)There are "large minded people who dream dreams as Dr. Martin Luther King, President Barak Obama, Hilary Clinton, Mark Kay Ash, Mary McCloud Bethune, President Abraham Lincoln and other great people with visions. (2)There are "Medium minded people" who thrive on events as NFL game, Essence Festival, Ebony Fashion Show, CPAC Summit or what happened at the Savoy Club last night. (3) There are "Small minded" people who spend most of their time talking about people like- the Kardashian sisters, the Braxton family, First Lady Michelle Obama, your sister or your best friend. Remember there is life and death in the tongue.

Have you met or do you know people in any of these categories reflected above? Let's not waste our time. Become a connoisseur of information. I agree wholeheartedly with the United Negro College Fund whose motto is "A mind is a terrible thing to waste." You cannot teach what you do not know. If you knew better, you would do better. Use your mind to expand or to acquire personal power. Have faith that Mr. Right is trying to find you. "You can be alright until Mr. Right comes along."

Let us hold fast the profession of our faith without wavering; (for He is faithful that promised). Hebrews 10:23.

For it is God who works in you to do His will and to act according to His good purpose. Philippians 4:13 NIV

WHO DOES GOD SAYS YOU ARE?

You cannot honestly express yourself until you discover who you are. It is important that you do not allow people to define who you are. Many people will try to use their personal power to influence you that you are not who you think you are. It is crucial that you know who you are and whose you are. I say ask God: Who do you say I am?

Some of your acquaintances will try to minimize you and make you feel you are not important or significant. You will have haters sometimes who will play mind games on you making you feel that you are the "scum" at the bottom of the barrel. Men who were in relationships with you in the past may remember you "when" and be determine to make you never forget your past.

You are not less than because you are not in a defined relationship. You are not less than because you are single. You are you and there is no one else in the whole world exactly like you. You own everything about you- every part of your body including your mind, thoughts and ideas. When God made you He made you in His image and He did not make any "junk or mess."

Being human means we all have strengths and weaknesses. It is always to our advantage to recognize our strengths and weaknesses. This is all a part of knowing who we are. We all fall short of the glory of God. Therefore, do not be so hard on yourself because we all are a "project" in progress. God is the potter and we are the clay. Let's give God permission to have His way. Even if we do not give God our permission- "God's divine will for you shall be done!"

How much value do you place on who you are? Are you less of a person because you are not with Mr. Right? Do you feel loveable and worthwhile? Are you depressed because you are not dating? Are you involved in an abusive relationship because you fear Mr. Right will never come along? Are you living with a man and refuse to speak about marriage because you fear this man will leave you or a conversation about marriage will drive him away from you? Do you place your life on hold waiting on Mr. Right to come along?

But ye are a chosen generation, a royal priesthood, a holy nation, a peculiar people; that ye should shew forth praises of him who hath called you out of darkness into his marvelous light. 1 Peter 2:9

The strategy of the devil is to convince you that you are not who God says you are. The devil comes to rob, steal, kill and destroy. The devil wants to abort your destiny. The devil wants to make you believe you are nothing because you are not in a relationship and you are not married. The devil wants you to believe that it is not alright to be alone. The devil convinces us to sin and get a little sex to appease our flesh until we get married. Then you give in to your desires and Satan beats you up making you feel guilty, condemned, filthy, broken, disgusted, depressed and oppressed.

Believe who God says you are. Rebuke the devil and he will flee. It is sometimes difficult to overcome temptations. Be aware! I say the only way to overcome temptation is to die to flesh and to love God more than you love yourself. God has called you and me royalty. Speak the word of God daily in your own life.

You cannot always wait on the preacher, evangelist, prophet or prophetess, spiritual teacher and apostle to speak in your life in Sunday church service. The preacher may not be able to connect to you when you have been kicked or beaten. You have to read the Word of God and bury it in your mind and heart and speak the Word daily to yourself.

Verbally confess what the Word of God says you are. Always remember you are a spiritual being, in a physical body embarking on a spiritual journey to reach your destiny which God has ordained for you.

I am not so concern what your name is. I do not care if you name is Faye, Josephine, Nancy, Alice, or White Diamond. God says you are fearful and wonderfully made in His image. You are Daddy (God's) girl. You are the apple of God's (our Father) eyes. You will not know who you are until you know who God is. "You can be alright until Mr. Right comes along."

Who shall separate us from the love of Christ? Shall tribulation, or distress, or persecution, or famine, or nakedness, or peril or sword? As

it is written, for thy sake we all the day long; we are accounted as sheep for the slaughter. Nay, in all these things we are more than conquerors through him that loved us. For I am persuaded, that neither death, nor life, nor angels, nor principalities, nor powers, nor things present or things to come. Nor height, nor depth, nor any other creature, shall be able to separate us from the love of God, which is in Christ Jesus our Lord. Romans 8:35-39

Before you give yourself to a man, get to know who you are. Get to also know who God say you are. Get to know who God says you are before you say "I do." What will you give to a man when you do not know who you are?

Let's keep it real because God is listening to you. Learn to operate with a single focus of identity-who God says you are versus who the world says you are. Listen to who God says you are and practice operating with clarity based on who the word of God says you are. People will treat you the way your inner wave connects to them.

Stay connected to the source-God. God is the vine and you are the branch. When the branch is disconnected from the vine, it will look alive for a period of time. Soon the branch will wither, appear to be dead and will actually die. Throw the branch in the fire. This is about all the good it is worth. If you stay connected to God, you can do all things. If you disconnect from God you are worth nothing.

I challenge you to spend more time with Him and not them. Get off the phone and go to the throne. Please do not get caught in habit of allowing others to commit identity fraud in your life. You are too valuable. Do not allow anyone to steal your identity telling you who you are, what you are going to do/not do or making you feel less than the woman God says you are.

Many sisters avoid self –awareness- running from themselves. Single people should first date themselves. If you do not enjoy your company, you do not have self- awareness or positive self-esteem. Therefore, you do not have a personal plan for your life to help you in your life journey. Remember, "You can be alright until Mr. Right Comes along."

SISTER IT'S OK TO LOVE YOURSELF

How do I look? Look in the mirror and began to like what you see because if you do not you will never be free. What do you see when you look in the mirror? Do you see an attractive woman or an unattractive woman? Do you see big hips, heavy thighs or thick lips? Do you see long hair, short hair or kinky or nappy hair? Do you see 36-26-38 or do you see 48-40-52.

There is only one you and only one me and God has designed us the way He wanted us to be. Some things you can change and others things you can rearrange, but accept the fact that you are a designer original that God has put on the rack and He gave you the confidence to change the things that you lack. When we look at ourselves and at one another, are we really seeing what make each of us so unique and special?

Have you ever looked in someone driveway, checked out someone car and said why can't I get a car like that? Have you glanced at some other woman's Coach Handbag and said I am going to buy a Coach handbag today? Have you eyed a sister's beautiful figure or coveted her man and thought, Man she has got it all? You have to watch saying if only I had a new house, new job, or a new man I will be happy.

You are beautiful! Please do not say "I am ugly." "I am stupid." "No man wants a woman like me." "Nobody likes me." These phrases speak of a negative picture of oneself. The way you think of yourself also determines how well you will achieve you goals in life.

As a young girl, I can remember people saying she is light skinned. She has long pretty curly hair. Today, we are bombarded with varied messages about what we should look like. Have you heard the conversations about someone who was too skinny, too fat, too black, too light, too thick-lipped, too wide nose, too nappy or kinky hair?

Too many of us are caught up in who society says we should be. Too many never see the beauty reflected in the mirror because we are determined we should be a size 8 and not size 18. Hill Harper says, "There are many women who, instead of loving their bodies, seems to be in love with what their bodies can get them."

I have a special male friend whom I have known for over thirty years. We often enjoy dinner together. During dinner, he talked to me about his views about some of the women he has observed. He stated too many women get too caught up in how beautiful they are, but that they never focus on intrinsic qualities like character. In essence, he is stating women should love themselves totally- inside and outside.

Your body is the temple of the Holy Spirit. There is a lot you can do with your hair, nails, and your body figure (losing weight or gaining weight). At the end of the day, it is necessary that you love you. Be the woman you want to be. All that God created is beautiful.

Whose adorning let it not be that outward adorning of plaiting the hair, and wearing of gold, or putting on apparel; But let it be the hidden man of the heart, in which is not corruptible, even with the ornament of a meek and quiet spirit, which is in the sight of God of great price. 1 Peter 3: 3-4.

We have to be careful what we say in nurturing and raising our children. Children remember words which are spoken to them. These words often linger as children grow up to be adults. It is a gift to show children that they are special. It is essential to show children that they are loved so that they can see their positive qualities-reinforcing them with words and actions. Never tell a child she/he is ugly. Never tell a child you are just like your "no good" daddy. Never tell a child you are nothing and you will never be anyone worthwhile.

Self- hatred is a heavy burden. Poor self- esteem often is reflected in the whole dynamics of the male/female relationship. What we do in pursuing or waiting on Mr. Right often is affected by what we feel about ourselves. Do we love or hate ourselves? What type of Mr. Right or Mr. Wrong we will accept in our lives?

Love yourself and please do not wait on a man to love you first. You teach a man to love you by the way you love yourself. If you want a diamond ring, work and save your money and buy yourself a diamond ring. You will be surprised how wonderful you will feel. If you want a car, a new dress, or flowers, you can purchase these items for you. The man will see how you love yourself. Do not set yourself up believing that a man loves you when he buys you things. This could be trappings to trap you. This is a valuable lesson to teach our daughters and sons. Live by the examples you demonstrate in life.

Sometimes, you must remove yourself from those people who speak negatively and behave wrong toward you. Be happy with you. Learn to love yourself. Enjoy your small and great achievements. Set aside time to think about yourself and the wonderful person you are. Remember, "You are somebody!" It is alright to love you! It is fantastic to be good to you. It is in Divine order that you take care of you! Your body is the temple of God. Remember, "You can be alright until Mr. Right comes along."

Ye are of God, little children, and I have overcome them: because greater then He that is in you, than He that is in the world. 1 John 4:4

YOU ARE SOMEBODY

Look in the mirror, I hope you like what you see.
Liking who you are will set you free.
You are somebody who God made in His image.
He did not make any junk and this is no pretense.
You are somebody!
There is only one you, so love the person God created you to be.
Everyone is special in their own unique way.
You may be single and alone right now but remember,
You are somebody!
You may be 50 pounds overweight or 50 pounds underweight,
You are somebody!
Your hair may not be as long or thick as you want it to be,
You are somebody!
You may be Black, White, Hispanic, Asian American, Native American
or Mixed Race,
You are somebody!
You may be broke, busted and disgusted,
You are somebody!
You may have been rejected and feel stressed, depressed and oppressed,
You are somebody!
You are a child of God-one of His greatest creations- you are a designer's
original.
Acknowledge the good in your life and offer the universe the gift of a
grateful heart!

Birds of a Feather Flock Together

WHAT IS A REAL FRIEND?

In relationship with a man, it is very important that you be friends first. As you grow older each day, physical features will change. Circumstances and situations will also change but God will not change. Friendship will last when physical features and circumstances change.

Slow the process down and be a friend. A friend will stick by you closer than a sister or brother. A friend is someone who knows you fully and accepts you completely. A friend is someone who accepts you holistically and someone who appreciates your weight, ethnicity, the size of your hips, the bigness of your lips, and the length of your hair. He/she does not try to make you over.

A friend is someone whom you can share your deepest hurts with. A friend does not gossip and share your business with the world. When you share your deepest innermost self with a friend, he does not see your weakness and try to take advantage of you by manipulating and intimidating you.

A friend is someone who will listen without lecturing. This friend will not try to make you feel inferior (small) at the expense of making himself feel superior (large). A friend will comfort you without condemning you. A friend will encourage you without criticizing.

Yes, a true friend is someone who will defend you when you are not around. A friend is not a "two faced person" who speaks positives in your life in front of you, but when you are not around your friend speaks about the negative occurrences and circumstances in your life. You do not want to be a drama queen or embrace friends who are drama queens or kings- always keeping something negative going on.

Do not be deceived: evil communications corrupts good manners. 1 Corinthians 15: 33

A friend is someone who celebrates you and not tolerates you. A friend is someone whose greatest joy comes from your happiness. Have you had a friend that when you share your negative circumstance, he starts to brag about his promotion or new woman in his life?

Friendship moves a friend to watch out for your well-being even at the potential risk of his own. He is considerate of you and your feelings. It is not all about him. A friend grieves when you are grieved, rejoices when someone special comes in your life and bleeds when you are wounded.

Sometimes in life, we grieve when friends leave us. Some people enter our lives for a season or for a reason. When Johnny enters your life, you should receive him as a gift understanding that some connections simply were not meant to last forever. The cheating boyfriend and the disloyal friend all have their purpose. It is critical that we not focus on the betrayal but on learning the life lessons they bring. When the student of life is ready, the teacher will appear. The cheating boyfriend could very well be the teacher.

Let's be real. Not everyone who comes into our lives mean us well. We must daily strive to consult with God about potential friends and our romantic prospects. God knows all things. God is everywhere. God is the alpha and the omega. God knows the beginning and the finish of all things. God never fails. If we let God do His perfect work, we will never fail to associate with the right people at the right time.

I have friends who I have known for twenty and thirty years. While there will always be a few people I can count on for the long haul, success in relationships does not always mean that friendship will last forever. Sometimes, you have to say good-bye to someone you care about, releasing them with love.

In the dynamics of the male/female experience, often men want to say that the two of you are just friends. He wants the fringe benefits of eating the cake and the ice cream too. Yet he claims you are just friends. Be mindful of the type of ID a man places on your relationship. When a man in your life kisses you, the two of you have crossed the line of friendship. You are now moving into a more intimate and romantic relationship. Be very clear on this and make sure that you and your friend are on the same page.

Be conscious that it is not necessary to have fifty or one hundred friends. Be selective in who you call your friend. You may only have enough friends to count on one hand-five or less. However, I would rather have four (4) quarters than 100 pennies. Real friends are rare, perhaps, because the key to finding a friend is becoming a friend.

Friendship is costly, demanding sacrifice and sensitivity, but that's what makes it precious. Have you discovered the priceless treasure of finding –or becoming a friend? A friend in need is a friend indeed! Remember when Jesus Christ is your best friend it makes us a better friend. "You can be alright until Mr. Right comes along!"

To Thine Own-self Be True

THE COMPANY YOU KEEP

We need to take a close look at our mindset and feelings about being alone. Sometimes, it is actually better to be alone than to be in the wrong company. You probably have heard the saying, "I can do 'bad' by myself." This phrase focuses on whether it is better to be with another individual or be by yourself.

Introduce to me you best friends and I will tell you who you are. You are known by the people you 'hang' with. If you run with dogs, you will learn how to bark. If you run with chickens, you will not fly. If you run with the eagles, you will learn how to soar. It is interesting to note that eagles fly alone and not in a pack. Eagles soar along and soar to great heights. As a matter of fact, eagle can soar above the storm.

Be not thou envious against evil men, neither desire to be with them. Proverbs 24:1

Have you heard birds of a feather flock together? Have you heard association brings about assimilation? You are really known by the company you keep. A mirror reflects a woman face, but who she is really is shown in the friends she chooses. A life lesson for you to consider is: You become like those people you choose to associate with- good or bad company.

Make no friendship with an angry man; and with a furious man thou shalt not go. Lest thou learn his ways, and get a snare to thy soul. Proverbs 22:24-25

Choose your friends wisely. The less you associate with negative company, the more your life will improve. If you decided to settle for Mr. Right who is negative company or association, it increases negatives in your life.

As you grow, your associations will change. Some of your friends will not want you to move away from them. Some of your friends will leave or reject you because they will feel you are now too uppity or think you are now better than them. They will want you to stay locked in the mindset where they are. Friends that do not want to see you climb or fly will want to see you crawl and fall. Your friends will either enhance your vision or choke your dreams.

He that walketh with wise men shall be wise: but a companion of fools shall be destroyed. Proverbs 13:20.

Have you encountered friends who seem to be about a lot of drama? Do you allow your friend's drama to impact or affect your life? Be mindful and always remember drama does not just walk in your life. You either create the drama in your life; you invite drama in your life or you associate with people that bring drama in your life. Watch the company you keep!

Depart from me, ye evildoers; for I will keep the commandments of God. Psalms 119:115

Let me tell you a secret. If women will raise their standards, men will raise their standards as well. Every man I know from ten to seventy years of age, who loves women, their "elevator" goes to the top, their manhood will embrace womanhood in terms of establishing a relationship.

When we think of raising our standards, often we think in monetary terms. A standard is a rule or principle that is used as a basis for judgment. Standards reference our morals, ethics, and customs in regard to an individual being acceptable or unacceptable.

What is acceptable or unacceptable to you as a woman? If women will raise their standards in terms of what in acceptable or unacceptable behavior, men will raise their standards. A man will be moved to desire a woman at some point in his life. If women standards are such to accept or reject men behavior or actions, men will be moved to develop a certain set of standards and behavior. This is so powerful. Women have power. No nation can rise any higher than its women.

I know many women struggle with whether their standards are too high when considering a mate or significant other. You will not find a perfect individual or mate on this earth. You, your girlfriends, your boyfriends or the other are not perfect. We all fall short of the glory of God. A compromise is allowing yourself to connect and welcome friends who have similar values as you. They value and desire what you want in life. If you value spiritual growth and development, you would want to connect and relate to someone with equal values. This is a part of being equally yoked.

You should consider whether or not a friend is adding or multiplying in your life. You should consider if your friends are subtracting from or dividing your life. Which friends would you choose? Those friends that do not increase you will surely decrease you.

Wait until Mr. Right comes along who can enhance your life. Wise is the woman who strengthens her life with the right friendship. Until that time wait on the Lord. God is too wise to make a mistake. He wants to bless you with the true and not the fake Mr. Right. God can equip you with the power of discernment to know this is the one. Until that time wait on the Lord. "You can be alright until Mr. Right comes along."

LET'S REMOVE THE LABELS

Just because you are alone, not in a relationship, not married and sometimes alone, please do not let others define who you are by attaching labels to you. You have the power to change the labels. Isn't that something, do not give your power to anyone by allowing them to say who you are?

We all have experiences, some positive and some negative, but you still do not have to allow your experiences, hurts, or wounds to define who you are. You may have experienced rejection, abuse, brokenness, and daily problems in your life. You could have engaged in toxic relationship which you know you should have gotten out of but was not strong enough to do so.

You could have acquired or heard of some of these labels attached to your personhood: whore, easy, cheap, desperate, old maid, the "B" word, slut, street woman or gold digger. You have the power to change these labels through your action and knowing and believing the Word of God. Ask again, God who do you say I am? God says you have royal blood flowing through your veins. God says He loves you so much that He gave His only forgotten son to die that you are good enough to be reconciled back to God. God says you are fearfully and wonderfully made.

As a motivational speaker, a few years ago I conducted a seminar for youth. I asked the females to identify males and the males to identify females in their lives. Below are the labels they could identify with:

Females (Referencing Males)	Males (Referencing Females)
Dawgs (Dogs)	Whoremongers
Snakes	Hoes
Bastards	Bitches
Punks	Gold Diggers
Faggots	Tricks
Sissies	Hookers

Cowards	Sluts
Convicts	Tramps

Therefore, drop the negative labels and replace them with what the Word of God says you are.

We can no longer think it is alright for men to engage in negative behavior and still be regarded as a "prize possession." We have to drop the double standards that it is alright for men to engage in negative unacceptable behavior but a woman must carry herself as a lady. Men and women must raise their standards as individuals so we can experience stronger families and communities.

But if we walk in the light, as he is in the light, we have fellowship one with another, and the blood of Jesus Christ his Son cleanest us from all sin. 1 John 1:7

If we confess our sins, he is faithful and just to forgive us our sins, and to cleanse us from all unrighteousness. 1 John 1:9

Replace those negative labels with positive affirmations. "I am loved by God. I am beautiful and made in the image of God. God has made me a good woman and He created a good man for me. The negative experiences I encountered in my previous relationships, God is using those experiences for my good. If it be the will of God, my husband is on his way to find me." Do not give up. God can give you grace (unmerited favor) to endure each day. God will not put any more on you than you can bear. "You can be alright until Mr. Right comes along."

For the grace of God that brings salvation has appeared to all men. It teaches us to say "No" to ungodliness and worldly passions, and to live self-controlled upright and godly lives in this present age, while we wait for the blessed hope-the glorious appearing of our great God and Savior, Jesus Christ. Titus 2:11-13 NIV

STRAIGHT TALK TO PLUS SIZE SISTERS

I have seen beautiful women who are slim or plus sizes. Today too many images depict desirable women as slim figures. Plus size women often get a negative rap about their "desire-ability." Many plus size women express that they feel they have not met Mr. Right because they are plus size. Let me tell you men appreciate full- size women. I have heard men say full sized women have a certain stride about them. Some men express they like the way a full size sister moves when she walks. Therefore, please do not believe all the hype.

Society has us thinking that anyone above size 8 is overweight and not attractive. I must confess I am a plus size woman and I do not look at my size as a negative attribute. I admit before having children I was smaller than I am now. I also have to let you know I have always had men around the world admire me. I have always focused on expressing my total holistic package- my physical, mental, emotional, social, and spiritual qualities. Express yourself! You can express your originality with confidence.

I am not trying to start a "war" with slim and plump figure women. I firmly believe that you do not have to be unhealthy just because you are pleasantly plump. You should always be concerned about your health but slim women may have issues with their health as well. Yet each woman must deal with her insecurities. You have to be confident and not to feel threaten by a female of a smaller size. One brother stated there is absolutely nothing "more sexier" than a woman who has curves in all the right places.

Plenty men are turned on by a voluptuous physique. Plus size women are attractive as seen in the physical appearance of Oprah Winfrey, Hillary Clinton, Jill Scott and Cathy Hughes. The flip size to consider is to love who you are and not get caught up in what society says. On the flip side, many slender women are often preoccupied with fitting society's standards for the "trophy wife."

We have to learn to celebrate ourselves. Catch a glimpse of your authentic self and discover the positive attributes about y-o-u. "I am a plus size woman who is positive and upbeat." I am a voluptuous sister who enjoys my gifts as a motivational speaker, spiritual teacher, author, life coach and jewelry maker." "I am in the flow of life and loving it."

Plus size women should keep an open mind. If a woman does not possess a positive body image- and many of us do not-learning to love your body can help a woman develop one. It is time for plus size women to realize that until we work on enhancing our self- esteem by loving ourselves for the better in big ways. We must start by choosing to break the destructive cycle of unrealistic expectations, especially our own. You are encouraged to start today, shun the world's ideal of beauty, because it is constantly changing. Do not wait for the world to celebrate you.

Define what is great for you and forget about what is not for you. Instead of obsessing about a body that is impossible to achieve, begin to realize you can feel better about living in the body you currently live in. Always remember a woman's relationship with her own body is the most important relationship she will ever have-more important than her lover, her husband, her children her associates or Mr. Right. You are not your appearance. The question is does the world know this reality.

One of the best kept secret is more women than you know are going through procedures to increase their breast, hips and yes lips. I say learn to love the one you are with- YOU.

It is time for plus size women to look in the mirror and ask some important questions: How do I really feel about me? Did God make a mistake when He created me? Do I want to lose weight? Can God create a Mr. Right for me? Are you vogue on the outside and vague on the inside? Beauty is in the eyes of the beholder! Can you own your sexy curves? Remember you do not have to be perfect to be great. "You can be alright until Mr. Right comes along."

Know ye not that ye are the temple of God, and that the spirit of God dwells in you? If any man defile the temple of God, him shall God destroy, for the temple of God is holy, which temple ye are. ! Corinthians 3: 16-17

HOW TO LIVE ALONE WITHOUT BEING ALONE

Regardless to what you think, millions of Americans are living alone. Some individuals are enjoying living alone and many are not. Living alone can be difficult at times. For some women, especially those who are middle aged, loneliness can be a terrible problem because they thought they would never have to deal with it.

Appropriately fifty years ago, women married young. They went from living with their parents to their husbands. Many were concerned about becoming "old maids" (over 25 and not married). Some women thought loneliness was something to worry about when their children were grown and gone.

Statistics say people live longer when they are married. Loneliness can be viewed by many as a terrible state. Please be aware- you can be single and not be lonely; you can be married and still be lonely.

Many women react to loneliness in a passive fashion, waiting for someone to rescue them from their isolation. Unfortunately, this does not happen often. Even if someone does reach out to the lonely one, lonely people are so needy for companionship that their emotional demands can drive away potential friends or Mr. Right. This does not operate in the lonely woman's best interest. What this does is to initiate a vicious cycle in which lonely women become more withdrawn and bitter, making it unlikely that anyone will seek their company-moving Mr. Right far from reality.

I will not leave you comfortless: I will come to you. John 14:18

Living alone does not in itself produce loneliness. There are people living in isolated situations who do not feel lonely. Women with high self-esteem and a sense of self control over their lives function very well being alone. The remedy for being alone is self- confidence. Listen up! The key to living alone but not being alone is to use this situation as an opportunity for personal growth and development and a time to pursue options that previously were not available.

Women who are alone waiting on Mr. Right often complain about the time they have on their hands. The question becomes is the situation the problem or how you respond to the situation? The time you have is not to complain about. What do you do with the time you have on your hands? Time indeed is a precious commodity and the freedom to spend it in any way you choose should not be taken lightly.

If you lose a dollar, you may later receive ten dollars from some source. When you lose an hour, day or year, you will never regain this time lost. Use your time for activities that enhance personal growth and development-building your confidence and self-esteem. You can be alright until Mr. Right comes along.

Time is often a forgotten gift. Many women find the time they spend alone to go back to college, build their careers, write a book, enjoy a hobby, travel, go on a diet or join a health spa. Actually, if you are living alone or waiting on Mr. Right, there is no excuse for you not to do all the things you thought you would like to do- "someday." You can redecorate your house, plant a flower or vegetable garden. You can also do some volunteer work and get involved in community projects, mentor young girls or teach a class in your given area of expertise. The possibilities are endless. Make your dreams come true. The bible says without a vision the people will perish. Life is too short. Please don't cheat yourself. Make your time on this earth count.

Casting all your cares upon Him; for He careth for you. 1 Peter 5:7

Combating loneliness is not just a matter of filling all the hours of the day with more activities. Building a network of supportive friends is also advantageous. You can share special occasions and interests with supportive friends. We all need the emotional support that close friends can provide.

Let's deal with it. Some women view themselves and their lives as worthless without a male companion or husband. These women react to living alone by getting involved in various activities, with the sole purpose of meeting men and remarrying. They are engaged in a hunt for Mr. Right.

There is nothing wrong with wanting to get married. However, women who focus all their energies on the goal of finding Mr. Right set themselves up for rejection and disappointment. Because they undervalue socializing with women, they also miss out on the warmth and empathy women companions have to offer. Women can empower, enrich, and enhance each other lives.

I believe that in everyone's life, God intends for us to be alone at some point. You may be alone when you are young or middle age or older age. Interestingly, God will allow you to be by yourself so you will grow and be able to hear from Him. You can find joy in being along because when you are alone you can be more creative. The more you are able to be along joyfully, the more at ease you can be when you connect to someone special.

Sometimes when you are in the company of others, it may be difficult to hear from God. God is speaking to you right now. Too often we are so occupied and preoccupied that we encounter so many interferences. Can you imagine being on the phone and you hear static on the phone, it is hard to hear the other person on the line. The static in your life can be people, male/female relationships, music, gossiping, Facebook or YouTube. Move away and spend time with God alone. Spending intimate time alone with God is a key component in establishing a personal and intimate relationship with God.

Life lessons are truly a blessing from God. One lesson that I have learned is when you learn what you can live without, you are actually able to ask life for the very best because you possess the powerful gift of discernment. You develop patience that allows you to wait gratefully until the best arrives because you know the best is yet to come. You are able to create in your life the ability to make conscious choices- to accept or refuse.

Let's put this in the proper prospective. Let's see what it looked like in the beginning. God created the heaven and the earth. God later created man.

And the Lord formed man of the dust of the ground, and breathed into his nostrils the breath of life; and man became a living soul. And the Lord God planted a garden eastward in Eden; and there he put the man he had formed. Genesis 2:7-8

When God formed man and placed him in the Garden of Eden. Woman was not his companion. Man was alone with God and in the presence of God. Therefore women should observe whether Mr. Right is in the presence of God-**life lesson**. Let's not be in pursuit of a man who is bound by the world, and we later try to drive him to the presence of God.

And the Lord God took the man, and put him into the Garden of Eden to dress it and to keep it. Genesis 2:15

Therefore man had a job to do. Man had work to do. Sisters, men should have a job or have the attitude I am going to find me a job. He should not be satisfied until he gets a j-o-b-**life lesson**.

God is a good God! Before woman was created, God gave man the word. He gave the instruction and word to the man and not the woman. The woman was not yet created.

And the Lord commanded the man, saying, Of every tree of the garden thou mayest freely eat: But the tree of the knowledge of good and evil, thou shall not eat of it: for the day that thou eatest thereof thou shall surely die. Genesis 2:16-17

God gave man His word and instruction not to eat of the tree of knowledge-not woman. What is the word your man is giving you as a woman? How is your man guiding and directing you? Is he Mr. Right or Mr. Wrong? Mr. Right will teach you the word of God-**life lesson**.

And the Lord God said, It is not good for man to be alone; I will make him an help meet for him. Genesis 2:18

And Adam said, This is now bone of my bones, and flesh of my flesh: She shall be called Woman, because she was taken out of man.

Therefore shall a man leave his father and mother, and shall cleave unto his wife: and they shall be one flesh. And they were both naked, the man and his wife, and were not ashamed. Genesis 2: 22-25.

The woman ate of the tree of knowledge first. She did not get the instruction from God when man did. Why didn't man give woman the words of instruction God gave to him (the woman who he said is bone of his bone and flesh of his flesh)? Why didn't Adam and Eve communicate about this?

Now the serpent was more subtil than any beast of the field which the Lord God had made. And he said unto the woman, Yea, hath God said. Ye shall not eat of the tree of the garden? And the woman said unto the serpent. We may eat of the fruit of the trees of the garden. But the fruit of the tree which is in the midst of the garden, God hath said, Ye shall not eat of it, neither shall you touch it, lest ye die. Genesis 3: 1-4

Where is Adam when Eve is communicating with the serpent which is motivated by the devil?

And the serpent said unto the woman. Ye shall not surely die. For God doth know that in the day ye eat thereof, then your eyes will be open and ye shall be as gods, knowing good and evil. And when the woman saw that the tree was good for food, and it was pleasant to the eyes, and a tree to be desired to make one wise, she took of the fruit thereof, and did eat, and gave also unto her husband with her, and he did eat. Genesis 3: 4-6

Again why was Adam not communicating, protecting and directing his wife-**life lesson**? How could the serpent communicate with Eve and Adam was not present? Sisters, God has given us basic instruction of what our man should be. After all, God made man in His image and made Man His glory. He made woman man's glory. If a man is not in the presence of God, it may be good for woman to be alone. If a man cannot guide, direct, protect and provide for his woman; it may be good for woman to be alone.

You will be able to exercise the power of choice. You will begin to ask yourself very pertinent questions. Is it best to be alone or am I in a better position to stay in this relationship? How can being alone bless me now and in the future?

It is very important to understand that short term problem solving can create long term misery. Please do make quick solutions to long term arrangements.

There is no way to avoid occasional loneliness but it can be minimized by treating yourself to something special. It could be getting a facial or massage, manicure or pedicure, buying a special dress and getting a new hair style at a posh salon. Why not treat yourself to a banana split or smoothie. You can even make the smoothie at home and enjoy it in your favorite room in your house or maybe lounging on your patio.

One sister says she minimizes her loneliness by playing with her cats and dogs. Reading an interesting book can be a special treat. Indulge yourself in special music or video at home. You know how to nurture others; now is the time to learn to nurture you. "You can be alright until Mr. Right comes along."

BE HONEST ABOUT WHY YOU ARE ALONE

It is time to talk straight and be honest. When relationships do not work out, it is much easier to blame men than to ask ourselves: Is there something about me that I have not looked at yet? We may hear ourselves engaged in conversation like this: "Good men today do not exist." "All men are dogs." "You cannot trust a man today." Just keep your eyes open. Good men are everywhere. You have got to be the type of person you are trying to attract.

We often bring old baggage to new relationships. We are looking for the perfect man, so we overlook the perfectly nice man. We try to fix the man and make him to be who we want him to be. Quite as it is kept, there are no perfect men or women on this earth.

You will have to make some compromises in life. What habits do you possess which are tripping you up? It is often hard to see our own issues. In order to see our own issues, we have to turn over the stones that fear and insecurities breed and take a look within. When you tell yourself that the problem is "them" you rob yourself of your power to transform the situation. Take the log out of your eyes. You can't change others; you can only change you.

Have you had conversation with your friends and the main topic is men are all the same? Yes some men have their problems, but that doesn't mean we should buy into the notion that all men are players, on drugs, in jail, unemployed or into White or Hispanic women. We should not generalize to the entire population (all). We do not know all men.

Whether you are saying "All men are dogs, it is much easier to blame others than to ask yourself: Is there something about me that I have not looked at yet?" Check this out! The truth is, when we want a relationship with a man who is not ready to love us fully, it is a sign that we, too, are not ready and have some growing to do. "When the student of life is ready, the teacher will appear. Often this man becomes your teacher even if the experience is not positive.

To find a good man (Mr. Right), you must believe good men exist. Make a list of the good men you know. It may be just three men you consider to have good qualities out of all the men you know. It could be your brother, friend, father or home girl's husband. Next, think of the positive qualities of men you have dated. This helps us get in the habit of looking for a man's good points.

Do you want a man and later in the relationship you tell him you do not need him? Do you tell him "I am an independent woman and I do not need a man? I do not need you. This is my house." Being a self-sufficient woman is not a bad thing. But if a man feels that he has no place in your life, he has no reason to stay there. Please do not get so accustomed to dining alone that you forget to set another place at the table of your heart.

Ask yourself: Do you hold men at a distance because you try to avoid pain you experienced in a previous relationship? Are you bound by the memory of a negative experience? For example: the man you love got another woman pregnant. Often we pack our pain from one relationship and carry it with us when we move into another relationship (baggage). The new partner gets labeled with the old partner's mistakes.

Hurt women feel that if they let themselves get into a relationship, it will be like the last time. They feel they will get hurt just like the last time they got close to someone. They do not want to risk being vulnerable for fear of being hurt again. The truth is it is impossible to be committed, intimate and emotionally invulnerable. Remember, the strong shield that protects you from the devastation of pain will also keep love and commitment away.

If your hurts are deep, a counselor can help you to confront the pain. If your tooth hurts, you go to a dentist. If you have female problems, you go to see the gynecologist. Why when you have mental issues, you are reluctant to see a counselor or mental health professional? You can't heal what you can't reveal. You can't conquer what you are not willing to confront.

Do you want the man that you can't have? Do you say I want Barak Obama? He is famous, handsome and has lots of cash. Of course he is married and she has not actually met him, but he looks good. Many sisters start their "Mr. Right Must Have" list with a physical description. We check out his teeth and his body built and what's behind his zipper. I know one woman who said she will not date a dark skinned man. I know more than one woman who says she will not date a man who is shorter than she is.

Many women get caught up looking at the wrong qualities in a man and one day look up and say "He does not have a job and appears not to want to work." The man may look up and say "She does not know how to treat a man."

Many sisters are equally obsessed with how he looks on paper. Many sisters who have "made it" say she is only willing to consider a man who match her degree or paycheck- or surpass her. Many sisters believe the man should be doing better financially and professionally. Anything less, she feels she is "settling."

Too many sisters have been blinded by appearance; overlooking the man's true character. For many women a regular guy can't live up to their fantasy. She may find that the regular guy is a gem. To recognize those wonderful qualities, we have to pay attention to his inner qualities like maturity, love of family, spiritual development, etc.

We sometimes settle for a relationship that we say is better than nothing. Sometimes our standards are not high enough. I am reminded "that if women would raise their standards, men will raise their standards." Unfortunately, engaging in a "better than nothing relationship does not make for a long term love."

You have heard the conversation about not being equally yoked. You have heard your parents and the preacher tell you that Christians should not marry Non-Christians. Unequally yoke signifies an imbalance in two individuals' relationship. Please know just because you are "saved" and single, you are not necessarily equally yoked.

Sometimes you need to be alone to figure out your contribution to conflict in the previous relationship(s). Often times we go out on the town searching to find someone to feel the gap or void in our life. Time alone allows you the opportunity to find who God is and who you are.

None of us can afford to postpone our lives until some Prince Charming comes our way. I have seen too many women live in a state of suspended animation waiting for Mr. Right to come along. Life is too precious to waste. The right men are busy, involved and active in the world. And that is where women should be too- for our own sake- for our own happiness. You must be connected to someone you can connect heart to heart. "You can be alright until Mr. Right comes along."

Therefore I will look unto the Lord; I will wait for the God of my salvation: my God will hear me. Micah 7: 7.

WHAT EVERY WOMAN NEEDS TO KNOW

Men do not mind meeting or dating strong independent women. I have to tell you men do mind connecting to women who they feel does not need them. Men like to be in the company of women who appreciate and need them.

Women should be proud of their achievements. However, men do like women who talk about their material success. If a woman lives a splendid life, great! Yet if your life is defined by your PhD degree, your Mercedes or your million dollar house, this is a problem for most men. Men do not want you to elaborate on your material success.

Men are also turned off by women expressing they do not need a man to take care of them. Many women make the mistake by stating she is just fine by herself. In essence, her attitude is she does not need a man.

It is not a crime for a woman to desire a man to share her life with. It is healthy to desire companionship, a family, someone to help you feel safe, someone to take care of the car, someone who is willing to listen to your problems and offer tips how to fix your problems.

Men do not mind if you need them. The man who is truly interested in having a healthy relationship with you wants to take care of you and wants to be there to help you through the hard times.

You can still be proud of your successes. You do not have to dumb down. You can even share them with men. But you can be real by adding the "hidden truth." "God has allowed me to accomplish more than I ever dreamed. I still desire a special man to complete my life- someone who I can share my "mountain valley experience" with."

Often when a man approaches you, he just wants someone to talk with who does not have an attitude. He will watch your disposition and how you carry yourself. Are you approachable?

Men are like warriors. He is a conqueror. Men are like a hunter. He will approach and try to seduce Sally, Susan and Shanette. He is watching you and observes what you may think he does not notice. He watches your body language. He will check out if the woman is an easy target. He notices the woman who dresses seductively and dances like she is ready for whatever.

Needless to say, there are some men who are looking for a "sugar mama." You would want to walk away from men who are looking for you to pay the bills. A man should not seek a woman to financially afford his needs or wants.

Sisters, please be aware that every "sugar daddy" is not sweet. The so called relationship can turn bitter sweet. "Sugar daddies" may come bearing gifts- Dooney & Bourke bag, key to his car, two month rent for your apartment, grocery for your kids, manicures, pedicures and yes cash money. All these gifts make you feel the man cares for you. You may even think the man is in love with you and will one day be Mr. Right. You may think this man is taking care of you better than your biological daddy.

Ms. Right cannot be bought. He is trying to buy you with gifts and money in exchange for sex. Isn't that what prostitutes do? Some men are so clever they can get you to prostitute your body without you even being aware of his demonic strategy. The big question is what do you want from the relationship- a car, rent or do you want a commitment from Mr. Right. Every man who looks good or appears to be good to you is not good for you. Yes, I said it- walk away and tell him you are not for sale. Tell him you are more valuable than rubies and diamonds.

"Sugar daddies" are not Mr. Right. "Sugar daddies" are players who have observed what they think you need. They observe you with their eyes and definitely pay attention to your conversation. The player will throw the bait out there to you and see if the fish responds to the bait. He is a number one player. He could be making $10,000 a year or $100,000 a year. If he sees your need and fulfills it in exchange for sex, he considers himself a number one, genuine player.

Some women will settle for toxic relationship with a "sugar daddy" but not Ms. Right. Ms. Right is waiting for Mr. Right and until he comes she is prepared to be alright until Mr. Right comes along.

Women have to be conscious of limiting their dating prospects by skipping over perfectly good guys for less attainable ones. Often women have to be wise and adjust their priorities and focus on traits that are necessary for a solid relationship.

Sometimes, you may look at a couple and wonder what the man saw in a particular woman. You may ask: "Why did he pick her?" A man may look at a woman who is fun to be around; someone who is cheerful and has a great attitude; someone who is noncompetitive, smart and nurturing. He may not be interesting in how much is in her bank account or her credit rating.

You may need to take a look at the man who works as a teller at the bank, drives an Impala, and has family values, respect for you and is honest. The guy driving the jaguar may be handsome and earns six figures each year but he is a dead beat who does not take care of his children and do not respect his mother or other women.

I am not saying you should not accept a gift from a man. A man who gives you a gift can be Mr. Right. If a man gives you a gift, it is because he wants something. What is important for you to do is to let the man know what you want. Be very clear that the true gift you want is his heart, true love, a committed relationship.

Make it very clear that material possession is not your ultimate gift. If he is not willing to give you his heart, then please do not be afraid to walk away and wait until Mr. Right comes along. All men are not dogs. There are many good men ready to be Mr. Right if you would allow them. You can be alright until Mr. Right comes along.

BE ANXIOUS FOR NOTHING

Building Commitment takes time. As years pass and as the world turns, a single sister may feel as if time is running out because she has not met Mr. Right. I urge you not to rush things. For example, the longer you put off sex the better. It gives you time to know the other person. Sex can create an emotional bond. There are very few women who have sex with a man who does not get caught up.

Even if you do not rush sex, fear and panic can make us eager to have a man that we do not take the time to examine his real character. You may be afraid to ask certain questions. If you are looking for commitment, be willing to share your truths and ask questions. Is he married? Attached? Does he want children? What are his hopes and dreams? What was his childhood like? Does he have any personal issues you should be aware of, such as illness or STD? Too often, we are really into the guy before we feel ready to ask questions about the sticker issues.

I waited patiently for the Lord; and he inclined unto me, and heard my cry. Psalms 40: 1

We want the relationship to be right-right away. We work hard overtime preparing to meet Mr. Right. When the good man comes in our life, we often make the mistake of thinking that the personal growth is over. We think the hard work is over. Let me emphasize building a relationship is truly a labor of love. The purpose of an intimate relationship is not that it be a place where we try to hide our weakness. The purpose of an intimate relationship is that it be a place where we can safely let our weaknesses go and we can reveal our inner self.

You get training on your job. Why can't you get training on how to turn your single life into something special and rewarding until Mr. Right comes your way? I strongly suggest seminars, workshops, self- help books and yes counseling if necessary.

Are you willing to work for a good relationship? Are you willing to identify your stumbling blocks? Are you willing to let go of old relationship residue? Have you stopped looking for you fantasy man? You have to affirm that if your significant other does not grow with you, he can't go with you. "You can be alright until Mr. Right comes along."

I will not leave you comfortless: I will come to you. John 14: 18

You're Not a Game— Don't Let Him Play

STAGES OF A RELATIONSHIP

As the world turns, Mr. Right is somewhere in the world searching for Ms. Right. Now you have a better understanding about who you are, let's focus on the stages of a relationship. Often relationship appears to move fast. Some individuals feel internal and external pressure to move the relationship fast to the next level.

Nobody gets pregnant and gives birth the next day. Pregnancy requires time to go through the various stages prior to birth. Allow the various stages of the relationship to teach and instruct you. Having a baby is more sometimes than we can imagine.

Seest thou a man that is hasty in his words? There is more hope of a fool than of him. Proverbs 29:20

Flesh gets so excited that we make a commitment. We move too fast without counting the cost. Date a man not just for fun, excitement or sex. Date to see if this is the person you would like to build a lasting relationship with. Let's slow the process down and explore the stages in relationships:

1. Sparkle Stage: The relationship is at its romantic peak. Mates feel they cannot live without each other. During this stage, the man and woman are on an emotional high. This high feels like two individuals have fallen in

love which creates a high, sweet and many emotions with longing passion, fondness, uncertainty and wonder. This stage is full of romance. In the sparkle stage the couple feels closer together physically and psychologically. They develop growing "us-ness" in which the world is filled with two individual lovers. Both focus on each other merit and disregard the other defects; so both experience an overwhelming desire for closeness which temporarily blots out the fears intimacy might normally arouse in them.

2. Stage of Disillusionment: During this stage, mates are getting to know each other better and experience problems. Mates often begin to question if this is a positive relationship. "He does not make me feel as he once did." Reality is surfacing in the relationship. The couple is coming to grip with the differences which truly divide them. The question becomes, "What do I do about all the things about him that I do not like- things I can't change?" This becomes a real struggle. It is difficult to be subjected to someone else flaws and limitations without questioning the commitment to that person. This stage also means mutual disapproval because it is unexpected. The most concentrated dose of approval people can get usually comes when they are falling in love. A major proof of the rightness of the relationship is measured by how the partner "makes me feel." Gradually, the appreciation turns to criticism. Conversation shifts to you make me feel so bad. This stage is necessary because the reality is life does allow you to be in a romantic cloud forever. Life is a challenge, and love will have to find a way if it is real love.

3. Stage of Mutual Acceptance: Man and woman are moving to a place of assessing if this is Mr. and Mrs. Right. Mates see the positive and negative qualities and decide whether positive outweighs negative qualities. After assessing personal strengths and weaknesses, they decide to stay or not to stay in the relationship. In this stage, the couple has brought their expectations of the relationship into some kind of equilibrium with their everyday lives. Frustrations and anxieties do not stop, but they no longer trigger doubts about the future of the couple. Each has gained confidence that the relationship is going to survive the good and the bad times. Mutual acceptance is the product of good work. The essence of mutual acceptance is the knowledge that with one's partner there is no need to

rush or hurry. There is no need to have to sparkle. There is no need to be anybody but one's self.

4. Stage of Commitment: Man and woman decide to stay in the relationship for the long haul. The assessment reveals more positive qualities than negative attributes. It is becoming more apparent that God has blessed a very special woman with Mr. Right. Mr. Right is excited about finding his other "rib." The big question becomes: Where do they go from here?

5. Marriage: The couple is in love and wants to live together forever- for better, for worse, for richer, for poor, in sickness and in health until death due them apart. It is time to celebrate two individuals coming together in Holy matrimony.

You are encouraged to be a game changer. When you change your game, change your name. Please do not allow yourself to go into another game with the same name. Your name is no longer whore or slut. When you change, your name is changed- you are a new creature. Old things passed away and you are changed. You have a new walk and a new talk. Dress like a new woman. Act or behave like a new woman.

Align up your actions with your destiny. God is branding you. You should not have anything in your life that does not line up with your brand. Your destiny has to be associated with where you are going.

Always remember Mr. Right is somewhere in the world waiting to meet Ms. Right. You do not have to look for Mr. Right. He will find you. You can meet him at the grocery store, in church or outside mowing your lawn. Stop the anxiety attacks and enjoy the wait until he comes along. See the real man, not just the "wrapping." "You can be alright until Mr. Right comes along."

Being confident of this very thing, that He which hath begun a good work in you will perform it until the day of Jesus Christ. Philippians 1: 6

DO YOU NEED OR DO YOU WANT A MAN?

The earth is the Lord and everything that dwells within. God created people, places, things, and events. Too often our lives are so consumed with things which make it difficult for us to distinguish between our needs and wants. The United States of America has more shopping centers than high schools with approximately 2000 added each year. We have become drivers, television watchers, junk food eaters, mall shoppers, and throw away buyers. When we go to the grocery store, we are confronted with more than 80 different brands of cereals to choose from.

When one of my daughters tells me she needs a dress, I ask her, do you want a dress or need a dress? Learn to distinguish if you need a man. It is important that you do not appear needy in terms of a man in your life. Too often, we desire a man in our life to take care of us. We desire a rich successful man. Too many women compromise their personal growth and development because they are waiting on Mr. Right.

Let's be clear! Needing a man is like needing a parachute. If he is not there the first time you need him, chances are you won't need him again. It is not wise to try and program a man to be your "life line."

Remember, everything of high value you have to dig for: diamond, gold and oil. Hide and let the man (Mr. Right) find you. Do not dress to expose yourself to a man. Man loves a little to be left to the imagination. Men of value do not come easy.

Do not wait on Mr. Right to supply your needs. Man is not God. It is important to recognize our hierarchy of needs. If we understand the necessity to meet our lower order needs before meeting higher order needs, we will be able to understand the behaviors that drive or motivate others to act positively or negatively. In essence, putting priorities in order is crucial to differentiating our needs from our wants.

Our Basic Needs: food, clothing, shelter, love

Our safety Needs: security, orderliness, protective rules, risk avoidance

Relationship Needs: need to belong-family, friends, Mr. Right, group membership

Ego Status Needs: social reward, professional reward, self-esteem, and respect

Self-actualization Needs: personal growth, need to be challenged, need to be creative.

Self-actualization needs are the highest order in the hierarchy of needs. It is difficult to achieve higher order needs if the lower order needs are not met. Therefore, you will experience difficulty in achieving your relationship need (Mr. Right coming along) if your basic need of food, clothing and shelter is not achieved. Always remember, success is not measured by how much you have. Success is measured by how far you have come. "You can be alright until Mr. Right comes along."

Ask, and it shall be given unto you; seek, and ye shall find; knock, and it shall be opened unto you: For every one that asketh receiveth; and he that seeketh findeth; and him that knocketh it shall be opened. Or what man is there of you, whom if his son ask bread, will he give him a stone? Or if he asks for a fish, will he be given a serpent? If ye then, being evil, know how to give good gifts unto your children, how much more shall your Father which is in heaven give good things to them that ask him? Matthews 7: 7-11

STRAIGHT TALK ABOUT MS. RIGHT

One of the engaging conversations among women is how to find Mr. Right. However, I never hear women ask how do I be alright until Mr. Right comes along? In order to find success in life and love, it is necessary to be Ms. Right. I know Ms. Right has thought about the qualities she desires in Mr. Right. A major question is: Do you deserve everything on your list?

You say you want a man who is a man of God, handsome, generous, professional, romantic, and makes over $60,000 a year. But are these things you? Let me tell you if you want this package in your man, you have got to bring it to get it. Let me talk straight to you, sisters, either change the list or change yourself.

We all have strengths and weaknesses. This gives you an opportunity to conduct your personal self- assessment about Ms. Right.

Ms. Right is a good woman who is proud of herself. She respects herself and others. She is aware of who she is and whose she is. She does not allow others to define her. She neither seeks definition from the person she is with, nor does she expect others to read her mind. She is quite comfortable articulating her needs. She daily prioritizes, separating her needs from her wants.

Ms. Right is hopeful. She formulates her goals and is strong enough to work toward achieving her dreams. Ms. Right understands the power of love. She knows love; therefore, she gives love. She recognizes that her love is valuable and expect love to be reciprocated. Ms. Right does not take love for granted. She understands love that is taken for granted will soon disappear.

Ms. Right possesses a sprinkle of motivation and inspiration, and a dash of endurance. She has no problem helping others. She understands this life is often about someone trying to help somebody. She knows that she will, at times, have to inspire others to reach their God given potential. Ms. Right knows her past, understands her present and moves toward the prize of the higher calling-her future.

Ms. Right knows God and does not hide her connection. She knows without God she can do nothing. She knows that with God the world is her playground, but without God she will just be played.

Ms. Right does not live in fear because she knows God has not given her the spirit of fear but the power of love and a sound mind. Instead, she understands that her life experiences are merely life lessons, meant to bring her closer to self- knowledge and unconditional self- love. Ms. Right passes through mountain/ valley experiences and opportunities and comes out with new and renewed freedom.

During happy moments, praise God. During difficult moments, seek God. During quiet moments, worship God. During painful moments, trust God. Every moment, thank God. "You can be alright until Mr. Right comes along."

I beseech you therefore, brethren, by the mercies of God, that ye present your bodies a living sacrifice, holy acceptable unto God which is your reasonable service. And be not conformed to this world: but be ye transformed by the renewing of your mind, that ye may prove what is that good, and acceptable, and perfect will of God. Romans 12: 1-2

LET'S GO SHOPPING: DEVELOP YOUR SHOPPING LIST FOR MR. RIGHT

When you meet Mr. Right, this is a very important matter. Lives can be changed by this male/female encounter. Therefore, it behooves you to understand that poor male/female relationships equal poor choices, marriages, families, weak communities, unhappy men, women and children. Healthy male/female relationships equal strong families and communities. This is a serious matter!

What are the ingredients of a healthy wholesome relationship? In order for a relationship to be healthy and wholesome a man and woman must relate on five levels- body (physical), Mental (intellectual), emotional (feelings), soul (mind, will and emotions) and spiritual(energy,drive, motivation).

Do you shop for a mate like you shop for a dress? When you go looking for your dress at Target and the Target salesperson asks you: "May I help you?" What do you say? If you are like me, you probably say "No, I am just looking." What you are saying I will know the right dress when I see it. Will you know Mr. Right when you see him by looking at his external qualities-just like the dress?

Unfortunately, most relationships reflect heavily on the physical level. We tend to get interested in Mr. Right based on how he looks, how much money he makes, the kind of car he drives and how much he has achieved materialistically. Too many relationships are generated and endured based on physical attractions. "He is a hunk." "He is gorgeous." What is the" junk in the trunk"? We later wake up and recognize that it is not Mr. Right but we recognize we are sleeping with the enemy. We tend to view Mr. Right in term of "ribbons, bows and the shape and size of the box." We never look inside the box. It could be a diamond inside or an empty box.

For all that is in the world, the lust of the flesh, and the lust of the eyes, and the pride of life, is not of the Father, but is of the world. And the

world passeth away, and the lust thereof: but he that doeth the will of God abideth forever. 1 John 2:16-17

Lust not after her beauty in thine heart; neither let her take thee with her eyelids. Proverbs 6:25

Where do you do your grocery shopping? Do you shop at IGA, Publix, Save A Lot, Food Lion, or Dollar Tree? I say shop wherever you like. The choice is yours. I caution you to make a shopping list wherever you shop. The advantage of making a shopping list is to make sure you get every item on the list. You may get more than on the shopping list but you are definitely assured that you get those items listed.

The ingredients for a healthy wholesome relationship are intrinsic (inside). The following ingredients were identified by participants who attended various Male/Female Seminars which I have facilitated:

1.	Respect	16.	Gentleness
2.	Understanding	17.	Communications
3.	Honesty	18.	Humor
4.	Dependability	19.	Intelligence
5.	Romance	20.	Sexuality
6.	Spirituality	21.	Attractiveness
7.	Role Modeling	22.	Wisdom
8.	Kindness	23.	Financial Security
9.	Sensitivity	24.	Affection
10.	Love	25.	Flexibility
11.	Responsibility	26.	Supportive
12.	Faithfulness	27.	Reciprocity
13.	Maturity	28.	Ambition
14.	Drug-Free	29.	Quality Time
15.	Friendship	30.	Patience

There may be other qualities which you would like to add to this list. Personality, security, and love for children could be important to you. It may be important for you to add- has a job. Whatever is important to you please add. I vehemently encourage you to develop your shopping list today. It is important for you to assess if these qualities reflect wholeness: physical, mental, emotional, soulful and spiritual.

Remember, when you go shopping for apples or pears, you look at them and chose the apple or pears which meet your expectations or standards. If the apple or bears look rotten, you will not purchase them. I know you do not plan to take rotten apple or pears home. You have to weed through negative qualities in your mate as well. Choosing Mr. Wrong is not in your plan.

Values are what attributes are important to you. What are your personal values? You should desire to connect to a man with similar values. If you value a man with spiritual values, you should stop, look and listen carefully to a man who tells you he does not believe in God. You should want to run from men who reveal to you "warped values." Warped values like women are to be used. Warped values like women do not think you love if you do not beat them physically. Warped values like women want to be controlled. You should run from men who possess these warped values.

I have heard some women say: "A piece of man is better than no man at all." God is able to do all things. God can do everything but fail. You do not have to box God in. You do not have to settle for anything. If you are going to stand for something, you have to be against something. "You can be alright until Mr. Right comes along."

And he that heareth, and doeth not, is like a man that without a foundation built a house upon the earth; against which the stream did beat vehemently, and immediately it fell; and the ruin of the house was great. Luke 6:49

TIPS IN CHOOSING MR. RIGHT

Are you like Adam in the Bible who searches for companionship through the animals in the Garden of Eden? Will you bring home a beast to live with? Anne Landers blessed many with her advice column. She offered the following tips for women choosing Mr. Right:

1. You probably won't find Mr. Right in a bar. Try grocery stores, church, where you work or through a friend.
2. If he tells you he is married, he's separated or his wife does not understand him- he has TROUBLE on his forehead.
3. If he tries to move in with you or wants to borrow money, be careful. He may be a con artist.
4. If his family does not like him and avoids him, maybe you should, too. They know him better than you.
5. Check out his car. It should be clean, serviceable, and insured.
6. If he has children, decide if you want to marry them, too, because that is the way it will be. And be aware that they are a direct link to his ex-wife.
7. You do not need a man to be a complete woman. Choose the man- don't let him chose you. Be selective. No one has the power to make you happier than the right man or more miserable than the wrong one.
8. Find someone who laughs at the same things you laugh at. A shared sense of humor will make the good times better and the bad times less difficult.
9. If you want several children and plan to stay at home and raise them, choose a man whose skills and education will put him in a high salary category.
10. If you want a career, don't marry a man who hates his job. He will resent the time and attention you give to yours.
11. Two red flags: Does he have a short fuse and a hot temper? Is he hung up on his mother? These are two negatives that inevitable get worse after marriage. Both can be disastrous.

12. Don't get married because you are afraid to be alone. No wife is more alone than one whose husband pays no attention to her.
13. No matter how wonderful his other qualities may be, do not marry a man who has threatened, hit or humiliated you. In fact, don't go out with him a second time. Such a man is hazardous to your emotional and physical health and should be avoided like the plague.
14. Pay attention to how he treats his mother. Chances are good that he will treat you the same way.

But of him are ye in Christ Jesus, who of God is made unto us wisdom, and righteousness, and sanctification, and redemption. 1 Corinthians 1:30

I hope you review these tips with an open mind and heart. "If you knew better, you would do better!" You are encouraged to be wise as a serpent and humble as a dove. "You can be alright until Mr. Right comes along."

THINGS WE DO WRONG IN RELATIONSHIPS

If a man wants you, nothing can keep him away. If he does not want you, nothing can make him stay. There is no need to stalk him. There is no need to keep checking his cell phone to see who is calling him. We got to stop making excuses for a man and his behavior. It is important to take your "blinders" off. If we slow the process down, we can allow our intuition or spiritual awareness to kick in and save us from unnecessary hurt and heartache.

I cannot say it enough times: You cannot change another person. You can only change you. Stop trying to change yourself for a relationship which was never meant to be. Again slow down. The race is not given to the swift but to the one who endures to the end. Do not be anxious for nothing. Never live your life for a man before you know what makes you happy. Men can tell when you are trying to over compensate.

Do not get confused between a man's intent to be your friend or a lover. Once he kisses you, the two of you have crossed the friendship line. Some men want friendship with all the fringe benefits- sex included. If the relationship ends because the man was not treating you as you deserve then, no, you can't be friends. A friend would not mistreat a friend.

You deserve God's abundant blessings. It is nothing wrong with a man wanting to be treated like a king. You should remember every king deserves a queen- you. Do not settle. If you feel like he is stringing you along, than he probably is. Do not stay because you think it will get better. You will be very mad at yourself in the future when things are not better but worse.

Please avoid men who have a bunch of children by different women. If he did not marry them when he got them pregnant, he probably will not marry you either. As Beyoncé says, "If you like it put a ring on it." What make you think he would treat you any differently?

Do not let a man crowd you. Always have your set of friends. Remember he is not the full course meal- the meat, vegetable, bread and potatoes. He is just the dessert and you do not have to have dessert every day.

Maintain boundaries and set standards in terms of how a guy treats you. He can't treat you like he treats everyone else, especially if it is negative behavior. If something bothers you, speak up. You sometimes have to show a man how you deserve to be treated and how you deserve to be loved. Men treat women the way they do because women allow them.

We hope he comes equipped with positive assets because if you are like me, you do not want to train a man because you can't change him. Change comes from within. The only person you can change in a relationship is you.

I know this may sound strange, but you should never let a man know everything. He may use it against you later. Do not ever make a man think he is more important than you even if he has more materialistic things, more education or a better job. Do not make him your "little god". He is merely a man, nothing more and nothing less.

Never let a man define who you are. God has created a man just for you. Therefore, you do not have to borrow someone else man. If he cheats with you, he will cheat on you. If he is married, you do not need to date anyone else trouble.

You should not be the one to do all the compromising. You want a relationship which is reciprocal. It should be a give and take situation. You should not have to always be the giver and he always receives. Remember every king deserves a queen not a fool.

A man should not define who you are. You should not look for someone to complete you. A relationship functions best when it consists of two whole individuals.

Do not be so eager and available at all times. Men like to have a little mystery in the relationship. Make him miss you sometimes. A man will take you for granted if he always knows where you are, what you are doing and you are always readily available waiting on him to call you.

Get a life! Do what you enjoy by yourself or with family, male and female friends. Do not fully commit to a man who does not give you everything you value. "To thine own self please be true." You may keep him on your list but get to know others.

Make dating fun. You can learn a lot about yourself and others via dating. If you enjoy the experience and you learn something about yourself, your time has not been wasted. Dating can be fun and advantageous even if he does not turn out to be Mr. Right. "You can be alright until Mr. Right comes along."

Casting all your care upon him; for He careth for you. 1 Peter 5: 7

DO YOU KNOW THIS MAN OR THESE WOMEN?

Recently, my daughter sent me an email which revealed breaking news of a 33 year old young man who has 22 children by 14 different women. Just think about this for a moment. He was in court in one of the most expensive child support cases. He said he loved all of his siblings. Note he called his children siblings. He said he considered himself a good father. He said he just could not pay child support. He further explained that he was young an ambitious and "I love women. You cannot knock a man for loving women." He was asked: Do women like him? His response was women do not like him- women love him. He said having all these children help his family legacy to live on.

He stated that his criminal record made it difficult for him to find gainful employment. However, he plays the lottery as often as he can. Looking at this situation, he may end up in jail again. His children range in ages from 18 to infants. Based on his age, his oldest child was born when he was 15.

He has been super busy! The big question is what are these women (mothers of his children) thinking? It is very important that women learn to delay personal gratification and be alright until Mr. Right comes along. Women have to be held responsible for their behavior also. Accepting responsibility for your actions is a sign of maturity.

One of my friends, John, responded to the 33 year old guy with 22 children by 14 women: "Well this man says he dreams. I imagine his nightmares are filled with images of beautiful women all nude dancing around his bed waving hatches and knives. Dr. Vera, you may not want to hear this but my opinion, this man is only half of the story. He was in the court for child support- not rape. They need to video the mothers and have the mothers to attempt to explain their persistent stupidity. We are talking about women who lay down with a guy who already had several kids with previous girlfriends, who obviously had no inclination to keep a meaningful monogamous relationship, who has a criminal record, and not gainful employment. The inclination here is to ridicule this guy by saying his brain must be between his legs. But I would place the brain of females no higher. Women are to be held responsible for their behavior as well. If I was the court judge, I would order about 15-20% of whatever wages this guy earns and divide that between the 14 stupid ass females. If I had to guess a number of those women, I bet are not married either and have kids from other men."

I wonder about the mentality of the 14 different women cited in the true story above. I wonder what they are thinking. I wonder do they have any regrets. My hope is they will benefit and be blessed by reading this book. The million dollars question is if you are ready to read this book and you ponder with this reality, what are you going to do? How are you going to deal with the reality that you are not currently in a healthy relationship and do not have optimism for the future?

I say examine your life today. Deal with this reality. Admit the truth. The truth shall make you free.

RED FLAGS IN RELATIONSHIPS

God does answer prayers. When the timing is not right, God says "No". When you are not right, God says "Grow". When everything is right, God says "Go". We sometimes leap into relationships too fast. We begin to fantasize about Mr. Right. Let's slow the process down. You may have experienced meeting someone and you begin to feel rushed. Stop! Look! And Listen! Below are some of the "red flags" which you need to be aware of:

1. He lies and you become aware that he is not honest.
2. He is insecure and he wants to know your every move.
3. He is jealous and always accuses you of not being faithful.
4. He tries to rush you to make a decision before you are ready.
5. He wants to move in with you immediately.
6. He has problems with his mom.
7. He has several children by many different women.
8. He does not support his children emotionally or financially.
9. He is already in a relationship.
10. He is married.
11. He lets you know he never wants to get married.
12. He brings excessive baggage from previous relationships.
13. He experiences outburst of anger, violence and lacks self -control.
14. He has a controlling personality-manipulation, intimidating, threats, guilt, and bodily harm.
15. He is needy and wants to borrow money, request your financial assistance.
16. He has much drama in his life and there is no or little peace.
17. He is in and out of jail or prison.
18. He has character flaws.
19. He possesses negative, warped values.
20. He appears to be in hiding and never wants to be seen in public with you.
21. He is selfish and it is all about him.

Let us therefore come boldly unto the throne of grace, that we may obtain mercy, and find grace to help us in the time of need. Hebrews 7: 7-11.

22. He spends all his money on his desires and passions.

When a man buys himself lemonade but fails to buy his daughter or you the mother of his child lemonade, this man is untaught, selfish and just plain disgusting. I can give you example after example. It is so important that you clear your mind and minimize your pride and see the "red flags." You have to tell yourself: "I don't have time for that!"

When you began to feel a check in your spirit, pray and ask God to order your steps with his Words. Ask God to be a light unto your path and a lamp unto your feet. Ask God to guide, to direct, to protect, and to provide for you.

Humpty Dumpty sat on a wall. Humpty Dumpty had a great fall. All the king's horses, all the king's men could not put Humpty Dumpty together again. God can put you together again because He is the potter and we are the clay. Sometimes, you may ask God to change the situation, and He says no I am changing you. "You can be alright until Mr. Right comes along."

ARE YOU A "TRICK OR TREAT?"

Some of you might be asking, what in the world is a "Trick?" A "Trick" is a woman who gives her power to men. She is concerned about what a man can do for her. Tricks are women who are lost and are looking for love in the wrong places. Tricks give sex to get love. The flip side is many of the men called "Dawgs" gives love to get sex. Neither one has a clue as to what love really is.

A woman who is considered a "Trick" has no idea of why it is necessary to establish boundaries. Our boundaries are shaped by our morals, principles, values and character. In order to stand for something, you have to stand against something. You cannot dress to reveal, and you definitely cannot show everything. Women of character will not want to use profanity but a "Trick" will curse like a sailor.

A Trick sees men as all powerful. You know only God and Jesus are all powerful. A woman who tricks must reestablish how she sees men. "Tricks" must see money differently. How a woman acquire money is crucial. The "Trick" may respond: No money no honey. Many "Tricks" may respond: You got to use what you got to get what you want.

It really is a mindset. The Bible says as a man or woman thinks so is he or she. Change the way you think and change your destiny. A "Trick" is very manipulative and strives in trying to get something all the time. She uses her body and people to get things. Her favorite question is what is in this for me? A "Trick" has hardness about herself. She is indeed a gold digger.

The "Trick" really does not love the man. Her efforts are not with compassion but are actions to benefit her. The "Trick" may have four different men for four different reasons. #1 Man may the "fixer up" man. The #2 man may be the man she can communicate well with. She can tell him her problems and what she really feels. The #3 man is the one with the g-o-l-d (the money). The #4 man is the one with the body to make her feel good and he does not have to work or have any goals. He is there to give her real love which is actually false love.

I heard a minister testify that before God changed her ways. She said she had one man to pay her bills; one man to hunch; one man to lie under. She spoke of how evil preyed on the weak. She is now a powerful minister.

Mortify therefore your members which are upon the earth; fornication, uncleanness, inordinate affection, evil concupiscence, and covetousness, which is idolatry. Colossian 3: 5

None of these men have grown spiritual and she does not care. She does not have a clue. The whole "Trick" thing is set up by the devil to rob, to steal and to destroy her destiny. When the "Trick" meets a man, a hidden dialogue of thoughts occur which says I want something from you and I am going to have the upper hand. Believe me when a man gives you something, nine times out of ten he wants something in return.

The Trick" is not a whole woman- she appears to be ¾ of a woman. The "Trick" is looking for a man who she feels can be 1 and ¼ of a man. Is this real? A man or woman can only equal 1 whole person. Where can a woman find on this earth a man who can be 1 ¼? The "Trick" has some growing to do to be whole-spiritually, physically, mentally, socially, emotionally, and yes financially.

Many men will have fun with the "Trick." She has no rules, requirements, or respect for herself and does not make any demands on men who pursue her. He may brag to his friends and call her a "Trick" behind her back, but he will not take her home to meet his mommy. He finds great pleasure in introducing the "Treat" to his family. A "Trick" carries herself in a certain way which honors the power of men. She wants men approval.

The truth is we have "Tricks" on every socio-economic level-poor, rich, and middle income. We have "Tricks" in college. We have "Tricks" in the ghetto and in the suburbs. Are "Tricks" in church? You bet the answer is yes. We have disguised holy "Tricks' who sits on the front pew with their min-skirts crawling up their thighs. Her pastors, deacons and mothers of the church are all disturbed and distracted by her appearance and her demeanor. The holy "Tricks" will appear to get the Holy Ghost and shout Hallelujah, praise the Lord. She will sleep with the preacher if the opportunity presents itself.

Being a "Treat" is a woman's crown. A "Treat" is a woman of noble character. She is worth more than money or jewels. She brings her man and family good and not harm. She speaks words of wisdom. She has standards and requirements for her relationships, carries herself with respect and expects potential suitors treat her with respect.

Sister to sister I am not your enemy. I love all of my sisters. If you agree that you are "Trick", my advice to you is to speak power in your life by saying I can be somebody with God. Use your personal power and stop giving it to men. Your personal power can fulfill your needs. Get yourself a j-o-b and stop depending on a man to supply your needs. Put your faith in God and develop a personal and intimate relationship with God-our Creator, our Provider, our Protector, our Director and our Guider.

Being a "Trick" is a mentality. Respect yourself and be all God wants you to be. You were not born to be a "Trick". You were created in the image of God for a Divine Purpose. You were created to be a "Treat and not a Trick." "You can be alright until Mr. Right comes along."

THINGS YOU SHOULD KNOW ABOUT A MAN

When you first meet a man, the situation looks glitz bright and promising. But once you meet, past the first few dates and the initial glam or sparkle wears off, there are a few things to know before making a commitment.

The first question to get an answer to is: Ask your man if he is married or in a committed relationship. Some men will try to rush you before you ask about the women in their life. Some men will hide that they are married if they are unhappy in their marriage, or they want to have their cake and their ice cream too.

Be suspicious if your man try to obtain your number but does not offer his number. Trust your gut feelings about your man. If he appears to be hiding something, this can be a warning to you. It should raise some questions about his availability for you.

The second question you should ask yourself is: What are his intentions? Do not assume just because he is charming each time he sees you that he is in the relationship for the long haul. Sisters should ask a potential mate immediately what his intentions are.

The woman needs to know if what he wants is compatible with what she wants. Have a conversation with him as to whether or not he is seeking a permanent romantic relationship leading into marriage. It is advantageous to know if he is the marrying type. If he is looking for friendship or a romantic adventure, you need to know that also. It is best to ask rather than assume.

We often see the signs or "red flags" but we just want to believe this man is Mr. Right. Pay attention to how he refers to you in public. Does this man refer to you as a friend or the apple of his eyes-the love of his life? Do not be afraid to ask him where are we headed in this friendship?

The third question you should seek the answer to is: What is your sexual history? Yes, it is your business to inquire about your mate's sexual history, especially if you have an intimate relationship with him. I have to tell you many people will not be true about their at-risk-behavior. Therefore, it is best to protect yourself. Even if Mr. Right tells you he has not had sex in five years, it is best to protect yourself. If you want your man to be tested for sexually transmitted diseases, you should agree to be tested also.

Next, you should inquire as to whether he has any skeletons in his closets? Slow the process down and inquire about your mate's previous relationships. Do you see any patterns in his previous relationships which may manifest in your current relationship? Unfortunately, some men are not capable of giving or receiving love due to insecurities. As soon as they hear the word love or marriage, they run like you have a contagious disease. Please do not allow this revelation or knowledge to cause us to prejudge.

I know we are intrigue by this man. You still should get the answer to the question: Does he have a money problem? Many relationship problems and divorce occur because of money or the lack of it. Get to know what his views and habits are on savings and investments. Ask him if he owes child support and is he paying his child support? If he is not meeting his financial obligation in paying his child support, he most likely will not be financially responsible in a committed relationship or marriage with you.

There is a difference in inquiring about how your mate handles money and inquiring as to how much your mate makes money. Asking a man how much he makes can be considered rude. You would not want to be perceived as a "gold digger." You would not want the man to think you are more interested in the money than your interest in him.

You may feel this man is surely Mr. Right. You still need to ask does he have a criminal record. I know a woman who went on a date with a man and invited him up to her apartment on the first date. She became sexually involved on night number one. While she was asleep, the man stole her key and made an image of her apartment key. The next day she returned home to an empty house. He cleaned house taking everything he saw was valuable. Safety experts often advise women to check out their mate's past before getting involved. Do not feel you are being nosey to use internet companies and private investigators that will print out his criminal history. You would not want to prejudge this man but I encourage you to trust your instincts about your man. Ask yourself: Do I feel physically and emotionally safe with this man? Does he permit me to grow in the relationship or do I feel he is stalking me?

Does he love and respect his mother and other people in his life? How does he treat his mommy? Did his mom instill in him the importance of respecting other women? Does he refer to women as "Bitches?" The best way to get the answers to these questions is to observe his behavior with family and friends. We can fake it sometimes but we cannot fake it all the time. Take time to get to know who you are dealing with. "You can be alright until Mr. Right comes along."

Teaching them to observe all things whatsoever I have commanded you: and, lo I am with you always, even unto the end of the world. Amen. Matthew 28: 20

WHO IS PLAYING WHO?

It is not my desire to cause trouble but it is best to know who you are dealing with. It is important to know the tricks of the game if you are going to keep yourself sane and avoid a broken heart. You may want to play for keeps but he may want to play the game. When a man is not ready or willing to commit, these signs may give you a clue.

- He refuses to give you a home phone number. He is being evasive if he does not give you basic information as home or work numbers. He could be hiding the reality that he has a wife. A man often will not tell you because he does not want to take a chance that you will find out the truth.

- He is often late, cancels plans or rearranges his schedule at the last minute. Any individual may have to change his schedule once in a while but if this becomes a pattern, these are signs that he in unreliable. If he repeatedly disappoints you by cancelling dates, let him go.

- He is so charming and too smooth. He is actually too good to be true. We often overlook "Mr. Smooth" who caters to your every whim to try to get next to you. He will try to make you feel special to get you in bed. He wants your most valuable "diamond" –your body.

- He talks about the future too early. He tells you what you want to hear to get what he wants. He may talk about spending his life with you or marrying you. Men study women and many determine what is important to you and tell you what you want to hear which may or may not be the truth.

- He spends an extraordinary amount of time with the guys at work or the gym. A man shows he cares about a woman by the time he spends with her. If the amount of time he usually spends with you dwindles, this is a sign that something in the milk isn't clean. If a man loves a woman, he does not hang with the guys every night. Sometimes, this is an excuse to get with another woman.

- He flirts openly with other women. When a man flirts openly in front of you, this is disrespectful. If he does this when you are around, I wonder what he does when he is not with you.

- He does not answer the phone when you visit. This could be a sign that he is involved in an undercover relationship. Pay attention if he answers the phone in a hush tone or answers the call in another room. If he ignores a ringing call, it may means he wants to spend quality time with you. Try not to jump conclusion, he may not be involved with another woman. It is important to get to know whom you are involved with.

- He speaks disrespectfully about other women. Pay attention to how he speaks about other women in his life. If he disrespects other women, he will disrespect you also.

- He is not interested in what you say. During your conversation, he often clicks over and asks can he call you back or leaves you on hold for an extended period of time. This is a sign that you are not a priority to him.

- He is often short on money and wants you to assist him financially. When he never pays for anything, he is using you. Check him out. If he is a lifetime student but spends his spare time watching BET, he is looking for you to support him. If he really cares for you, he will collect his pennies and buy you a rose or a special card from the Dollar Tree.

- You become intimate with him but he continues to introduce you as his "friend." You do not sleep with your friends. You may be sleeping with the enemy.

- You make most of the phone calls. He calls only for sex. When he cares for you, he picks up the phone to call you. Do not be anxious. When you call a man more than he calls you, this is a man to avoid. If he calls you late at night-a booty call- this is a man to avoid.

- He does not want you to be around his family or friends. If this man wants to be alone with you in private but not in public, this shows you that you are not a part of his life. If he cares for you, he will take you to the movie, dinner with his friends or some event. Please be aware that meeting his family and friends gives you apparent insight into his character. He may be concerned that his parents will warn you who he is. I hate to be the bearer of bad news, but he may tell you that his parents died in a fire if he is an extreme liar.

- He is overly jealous or possessive. He falsely accuses you of cheating. This could be a sure sign that he is the one cheating because he is viewing your behavior through his values, and this makes him suspicious. He calls you every hour to check in or check on what you are doing. It may seem like love, but this can be a sign that you are dealing with an insecure person who will cause you grief in the future.

- He lies in front of you. When he lies to others in front of you and you laugh, you are a sick. He makes promises that he seldom fulfills. You cannot depend on him. His creditability and integrity are in question.

- He insists on sex now. Before he can get to know you, he rushes you for sexual favors. He knows sex will override your good judgment and make you blind to who he is.

- He wants you to invest in his get rich scheme. He knows he will get wealthy from his music deal and he does not want you to miss out. A premarital investigation may be worth investing money in. Check him out!

- You feel uneasy when you are with him. You feel insecure when you are with him and do not like the person you become when you are with him. What is your intuition telling you? I say your instincts are telling you to get rid of him.

It behooves you to be aware of the games. If relationships are about coming closer, than be aware games are about moving apart. Many play the "toilet tissue game." We need toilet tissue. We have to have it and we make sure we have it. However, when we finish using the toilet tissue, we discard it. Many people use you like toilet tissue and discard you until they are ready to use you again. They try to get the maximum benefit for the minimum effort.

Some play the "information game." Their goal is to get to know as much as they can about you but keep information about themselves to themselves-in hiding. When they gain information, they gain power and will often use information against you to control you and empower themselves. He does not easily share his past with you because he recognizes that information is power. Those people with information will control those who do not have the information.

Many take pride in the "disappearing act." He is with you and into you for a while. He later breaks normal behavior and patterns. Suddenly, he is not accessible and you do not hear from him again. Many men disappear on Valentine day, Christmas, birthdays and special holidays.

The "game of inferiority/superiority" motivates an individual to put you down to make you appear small (inferior) at the expense of making himself feel large (superior). This individual strives to keep you weak focusing on your negative qualities. You will not hear this "gamer" acknowledge his weakness. He will never admit he was wrong, and you will most likely not hear him say he is sorry. He will elaborate on your weakness because he wants you to know you are the problem. His goal is to keep you with a negative self-esteem which enables him to be in control. Do not get caught up in the game, he will steal from you while you are blind.

Stop! Look! Listen! We create this fantasy of love. Although we see the warning signs, we still go forward even though we know something is wrong. You need to make some changes to avoid being played.

Do not overlook the "nice guys." Many women today are drawn to the "bad guys." Often-time, the nice guys without the game seem somewhat boring. A nice guy gets classified as "friend" and the bad guy gets classified as "exciting."

We want Mr. Right to be a perfect spouse. Marriage is about connecting to someone with the same values and not necessarily romance.

Honesty is the best policy. Distance yourself at the first sign that he is lying to you. If he tells one lie, he will tell three lies to cover up the first lie. If he tells you a lie, the whole relationship is a lie. This reminds me of the man who did not tell the wife he had a son until the son was about ten years old. The whole marriage of fourteen years was a big lie.

I encourage you to become his friend before becoming his lover. Believe me a man respects a woman who does not hop in bed with him the first time you meet. He feels if you hop in bed with him on the first date, other men have done the same. He will have sex with you on night #1 but he will probably write you off, and he definitely will not take you home to meet his mommy or his grandmother.

Get a grip! Do not get hooked into believing the "boys will be boys" hype. Do not make excuses for man's infidelity. Do not excuse men from being accountable for their actions. Raise your standards and your expectations of men.

Do not be deceived by money, sex or gifts. This does not mean these gifts come from the man's heart. He feels he has the right ingredients to make your world go around. In essence, he thinks he can rock your world! He may think the right ingredients to trick you are money, jewelry, credit cards or lot of lies, lies and lies. Women think he is sincere because they play right into his scheme and games. The man thinks it is a winning strategy to show attention, and consideration. The woman will feel he cares. This is not necessarily the case.

Sisters, please do not let the "trophy man" fool you. Inspect the package by looking beyond what you see on the external. Do not get hung up on the image. Mr. Wrong can look the right kind of way, and you are anxious to show him off to your girlfriends. He wears name brand clothes, the right cologne and offer to take you to the right restaurant.

"To thine own self please be true." Many men will tell you he is seeing other women. Believe him because he is telling you the truth. Avoid this man like a plaque and do not get in a relationship with him. A woman knows when she is being played. I know this thing called playing the game brings hurt and frustration. You have got to be clear on what you will and will not tolerate. Do not ignore your instincts. Women who express their values, boundaries and self-worth are rarely mistreated by men.

Casting all your care upon him; for he careth for you. 1Peter 5:7

Avoid feeling needy or desperate for a man. Many women have been socialized to see themselves as incomplete if they do not have a husband, boyfriend or Mr. Right. Searching for a man to fill emptiness or void in your life is a recipe for hurt and disappointment.

You are in an advantageous position to find what your purpose in life is and to fulfill that purpose. Ask God what is the purpose of your life? When you find your purpose, you are walking in true abundance. When you find out what your purpose is, you find your provision. When you find a man to share your abundance you are more likely find the love you are looking for. It is worth waiting on Mr. Right. "You will be alright until Mr. Right comes along."

HOW TO AVOID MR. WRONG?

While you are waiting on Mr. Right, you will come in contact with many men. Some men you will decide to engage in conversation(s) with and some you may decide to date. It is crucial that you are informed so you can avoid wasting your mind and time on Mr. Wrong. Dating the wrong man is like eating a big slice of German chocolate cake when you are trying to lose weight.

Some people can be like eating pot ash or drinking bleach which will poison you. Some people can be poisonous to your health and well-being. Exposure to toxic people can lead to depression, anxiety and physical illness.

Ask yourself: Do you feel you are giving more to the person than he is giving to you? You give more and more, and he comes to receive. When you are around this person, do you feel physically and emotionally drained? When you are around this person, do you feel you focus more on his problems and most time it is not about you? If you answer yes to these questions, you are most likely dealing with a toxic person and it will affect your life in ways that you would not want to believe-you will become toxic also.

If you remain in a toxic relationship, soon you will experience a lack of balance. You will begin to feel like the person is a challenge to be with. Sisters, please understand that we are naturally nurturers and wired to take care of others. The problem is toxic people can take advantage of you and leave you feeling depleted. You are never going to receive as much as you give in the relationship. You do not have to feel trapped or controlled by toxic relationships.

Recognize the signs of toxic personalities or relationships. You have control over your life. You make decisions about who will be your friend or lover. He cannot take you if you do not allow him to. Toxic personalities are linked to depression, loneliness, and lack of self-esteem. Encourage this individual to seek professional help.

You do not want to lose your mind and health in the process. Most women have fallen for the game at some time in their life. If you overlook the "red flags" and fall for a man with hopes of adventure or sexual chemistry-believing you can make him change because you are a good woman, you need to get a grip and face reality.

Statistics show approximately 50% of first time marriages do not work; approximately 60% of second time marriages do not work; and approximately 74% of third time marriages do not work. Statistics reveal experience does not manifest constant or success in marriage. Tolerance actual appears to decrease over time.

Interestingly, many Christians feel pressure to marry to avoid fornication. Christian makes a very special attempt to get right with God but wrong with marriage.

Many women and men open their hearts but close their heads. It is important that your head and heart meet. It is okay to feel with your heart, but you also need to think about many things when you are on a journey to meet Mr. Right. Despite your honest intentions, it is never right to get involved with Mr. Wrong. Take time to see the secret baggage he daily carries around.

FIVE MEN TO MEET BUT NEVER DATE OR MARRY

As the world turns, you will meet many men. Some are to just be friends, some you will not want to continue to date and the following you should never marry. Just say hello, and good-bye could prove to be the best policy.

Mr. Player-Player

Let me tell you about the Player-Player. He is charming, sophisticated and fine as he can be. He has chemistry and you are drawn to him. The Player-Player knows he has it going on. His ego tells him he is a "gift" to the women of the world. He would not dream of dating just one woman. If you stay in this relationship, you will get burned-for real. The Player-Player has great social skills. On the surface, the Player-Player seems like Mr. Right because everyone likes him. He is confident and makes you feel that you are the only woman on earth. He will not reveal to you how many women he is seeing. As long as you are fun, the Player-Player will be around. The moment you start questioning where he was last night and why he did not call, you will begin to see his other side—the secret side. When things get tough, he will move to the next woman. You have to decide if you want to be the "table cloth or the dish rag."

Mr. Controller

This brother initially seems to be so nice. The Controller appears to be concern about you but soon it becomes obvious that he takes it to the extreme. He demands to always know where you are, who you are with and what time you will return. If you do not arrive by his specified time, he flies into a panic mode and may express anger. He desires to be with you 24-7. His fatal flaw is that he does not know how to separate love from control. The Controller is not independent enough to trust his woman so the two of you can have an adult healthy relationship. He is needy and he seeks the type of woman to take care of him and he wants her to be there all the time. He uses control techniques of manipulation, intimidation, guilt trips, threats and it could escalate to inflicting body harm. He needs to control in order to uplift or elevate himself. Please do not confuse his controlling behavior with love. God does not control you, but He allows you your free and permissive will. The big question is why would any man want to control you?

Mr. Abuser

This man is a possessive and jealous man who has unresolved issues and will physically and emotionally mistreat women. The Abuser will use insults to control, telling a woman that no one else will want her. He tells a woman that she cannot do any better. He may tell the woman no man wants a woman with kids. When a man has not been taught how to respect women, he is more likely to be abusive. Quite as it is kept, a woman in this type of relationship does not feel good about herself. She is suffering from low self-esteem. No woman wants to be abused, but many women fall into the abuse cycle and confuse abuse with love because the man later apologizes and makes her feel special. There is a problem in this relationship, and the woman will experience abuse, the honeymoon and abuse again: the verbal, psychological, emotional, physical or sexual abuse. The Abuser tries to apologize and next comes the honeymoon where he endears you with flowers, candy, new dresses or if he can afford it a new Mercedes Benz. The problem lingers and if not resolved, the abuse occurs again. Abuse is a process that will occur again and again if there is no proper healthy intervention. Never date or marry a man who makes you feel afraid. A man should make you feel secure. He should protect you and not bring harm to you or your surroundings.

Mr. Mommy Man-Child

Check out Mr. Mommy Man-Child. He is still living at home and it is not because he is taking care of mommy and daddy. The Mommy Man-Child is living rent free, eating chicken and rice and being spoiled. The Mommy Man-Child has no "get- up- and –go" and is not seeking employment. Mommy and daddy are supplying his needs, and he is not being encouraged to grow up and be an adult. The Mommy Man-Child is not capable of thinking for himself or planning how to make his independent future. He is not prepared to take care of himself because he believes that a woman should always be there to take care of him. He does not want to assume responsibility. The Mommy Man-Child looks for a woman to cater to his desires. He avoids committed relationships. He may seem to be attractive and fun loving but open the package and look at what is inside. The Mommy Man-Child is insecure, care free and lazy; so, let's not confused his fun-loving to be romantic and exciting. He has not learned that one of the signs of maturity is learning to assume responsibility for his own actions. He is depending on mommy, daddy and whatever woman agrees to be his lover.

Mr. Unsatisfied

He is never satisfied with the way you are and likes to drop hints about what you need to improve. He tells you he likes a woman with long hair. Mr. Unsatisfied tells you he does not like a woman who is plus size. He looks at you saying you can really stand to lose 20 pounds. Mr. Unsatisfied is not happy with his life and is critical of everything. He does not like himself and projects his insecurities onto the woman. He makes the woman feel responsible for what is not right in the relationship to keep from getting involved. If he is never satisfied, he does not have to commit. If he is not satisfied with a woman, he should find someone else.

We enter into relationships for different reasons. Women who find themselves with these types of men should stop, look, listen and run from these men. Learn to love and respect yourself so you won't look for external validation and settle for Mr. Wrong whom you should have avoided.

Abstain from all appearance of evil. 1 Thessalonians 5: 22

Sisters: Stop-Look and Listen

BROKEN SISTERS

When Adam and Eve were in the Garden of Eden and they disobeyed God, they hid themselves behind fig leaves. Many women today are hiding behind fig leaves also. How many women you know today who are hiding behind "fig leaves"?

Have you seen women who are broken but they are trying to hide their true colors? She appears normal at first but soon her cover is blown. Her passive-aggressive behavior, obsession with money and power turn from a sister who appears to be together to a sister who is broken into pieces. The following sisters' character flaws can be healed:

Ms. Gold Digger

All Ms. Gold Digger wants is what money can do for her. She is not interested in men who cannot do anything for her. She is going for the g-o-l-d. She feels insecure and needs material possession to boost her self-esteem. She believes she deserves a man who can shower her with cash, gifts and other finer things of life. She targets the rich and famous, professional athletes, entertainers or business men. No matter how much money is spent on the Gold Digger, she always wants more. She wants to be in the latest fashions, drive the best car, eat at the most expensive restaurants and take expensive exotic vacations. One sister Facebook name was designated as "Car Note-Light Bill." Ms. Gold Digger lives by the motto: "No money-no honey."

Ms. Rebound

Fresh out of a relationship, she is looking for a guy to fill the mental void left by her ex or a warm body to make her ex feel jealous. She is an unstable bundle of emotions. She rebounds from one relationship to the next. Her life is like a "roller coaster ride." She avoids being alone so she rebounds from relationship to relationship. Ms. Rebound bounces from relationship to relationship because of her insecurities. She fears being alone and feels being in a relationship with a man is the solution to her problems.

Ms. Drama Queen

When you first meet Ms. Drama Queen, she seems normal but after you spend some time with her you soon realize that she is unstable. She may tell a man I do not know what I would do if you leave me. She may cry without your understanding the reason. She may ask you to tell her that you will never leave her. She looks for a great deal of attention and feels that things have to be chaotic or she is not living. Ms. Drama Queen is running from something like disappointment in her career or even intimacy. She creates drama to avoid expressing real feelings or emotions. Rumors are that these overemotional women are great in the romance department. However, they experience frequent temper tantrums, create public displays of emotion and unannounced visits to someone's job where she picks an argument. Ms. Drama Queen may appear beautiful on the outside but is fighting an internal war.

Ms. Sgt. Major

All she wants to do is boss you around. She is always bossing someone around. Do this. Do that. Why did you do this? Ms. Sgt. Major appears to be a person who loves to nag. She has a need to take care of every situation. She will take a man's menu and order for him. The excessive need to make all decisions is based upon her beliefs and how she was raised. Ms. Sgt. Major gives the orders and expects others to obey accordingly.

Ms. Soap Opera

She attracts disastrous relationships usually because of the flaws in her personality. She has experienced much drama in her life. Anything that could possibly go wrong has happened to her. She has been there, seen that and done that. Dated an abusive boyfriend? She has been there. Seeing a married man? She has tried it. She often feels victimized and she gets pleasure by seeking sympathy and gaining support, attention and reassurance. She is the young and the restless searching for tomorrow.

Neither yield ye your members as instruments of unrighteousness unto sin: but yield yourselves unto God, as those that are alive from the dead, and your members as instruments of righteousness unto God... Know ye not, that to whom ye yield yourself servants to obey, his servant ye are to whom ye obey; whether of sin unto death, or of obedience unto righteousness? ... I speak after the manner of men because of the infirmity of your flesh: for as ye have yielded your members servants to uncleanness and to iniquity unto iniquity; even so now yield your members servants to righteousness unto holiness. Romans 6: 13, 16, 19

Broken sisters can change. I believe individuals only change when they want to or by an act of God. We cannot judge others. God is the judge and He commands us to judge ye not that we shall not be judged. Therefore, we should be a "fisherman" of women and men. God can change the Ms. Gold Digger and Ms. Drama Queen. We can love and mentor our sisters who are broken. We are our brothers and sisters keepers. I believe it just might be love that is needed to solve the conditions of this world. We can mentor our sisters and encourage them to know that "they can be alright until Mr. Right comes along."

ARE YOU ATTRACTED TO BAD BOYS?

Have you ever dated the type of guy that left you constantly waiting by the phone with an uneasy sick feeling in your stomach and would lie to you with a twitch of his eye? Have you dated or entertained a guy who disrespected you and made you feel bad about yourself, but for some reason you could not leave him? Have you ever walked into a club and you found yourself so attracted to the guy who looked like he had it all together but constantly used profanity and constantly flirted with every woman at the club, yet left you in a trance?

If you answered yes to any of the above questions, it may be a sign that you are susceptible to a certain dangerous personality type called the "Bad Boys."

I have conversation with many young and mature women. Too many reveal that they are interested in the "Bad Boys." Who are the "Bad Boys? The "Bad Boys" have no respect for a woman or the law. We wonder why there is so much drama in our lives. We are seeking men with negative warped values.

These guys have the tendency to be smooth, engaging, charming, and slick. They are not shy, self-conscious, or afraid to say anything. "Bad Boys" often have an inflated view of their abilities or their self-worth. They are self-assured, opinionated, cocky, and braggart. They are arrogant guys who believe they are a superior human being. In essence, they feel they have it going on.

"Bad Boys" have an excessive need for the thrills and excitement in life. They take chances and engage in things which are risky. Women often get caught up in this exciting roller coaster ride. They have low self-discipline in carrying task through completion because they get bored easily. To make it plain, they are not responsible people.

As you probably can imagine, "Bad Boys" can be shrewd, cunning, sly, and clever. They can also graduate to being deceptive, deceitful, underhanded, manipulative and dishonest. They use deceit and deception to cheat, con and defraud others for personal gain. It is all about them. They have a lack of concern about the feelings and suffering of the one being victimized. They have a lack of remorse or guilt concerning the losses, pain and suffering of victims. They are coldhearted.

They are parasitic in nature which moves them to be exploitative in financial dependence on others as reflected in the lack of motivation, low-discipline and inability to complete responsibilities. They will strategize for the woman to provide for them financial. They may sale drugs in the day but depend on the woman to provide a house for him to live in even if the woman is on food stamps. Yet, they say they love the woman. He is truly a "Bad Boy."

I have had engaging conversation with women who question whether some men love women. They indicate their experiences with men made them feel that men are their adversaries and not their friends. My question is do these men love themselves? If a man does not love himself, how can any woman expect him to love her? If a man does not love himself, how can a woman expect him to love his wife like God instructs him to? He should love his wife as Christ loves the church and love his wife as he loves himself.

"Bad Boy's" behavior reflects being out of control. They express irritability, annoyance, impatience, threats, aggression, and verbal abuse.

Be not deceived: evil communication corrupt good manners. Awake to righteousness and sin not; for some have not the knowledge of God: I speak this to your shame. 1 Corinthians 15: 33-35.

Because too many women are often caught up in sexual pursuit and fantasies, "Bad Boy's" promiscuous sexual behavior often becomes attractive. "Bad Boys" engage in brief, superficial and numerous affairs. They indiscriminately select sexual partners and maintain several relationships at the same time. Because they are "Bad Boys", they have a history of making attempts to sexually coerce others into sexual activity. They are very proud of their sexual exploits and spend time discussing their sex life with other "Bad Boys."

Ask a "Bad Boy" what are his goals? He has an inability or failure to develop and implement long-term goals. He has a nomadic existence. He is like the young and the restless, searching for tomorrow. He lacks direction in his life. Interestingly, if he does not have a plan, he plans to fail.

Women love romance. We must teach our daughters how to distinguish between a man who flatters her and a man who compliments her. Sisters sometime get caught up in the "Bad Boys" impulsivity. This experience seems exciting and seems so romantic. Their behavior is spontaneous, unpremeditated and possess a lack of deliberation without considering the consequence. They demonstrate rash, unpredictable, erratic and reckless behavior. Sex can cause blindness. Remember sex is not love and love is not sex.

"Bad Boys" engage in many short term relationships which indicate they are not interested in commitment or marriage.

Young or old, "Bad Boys" may engage in diverse types of criminal offenses and take pride in getting away with crimes.

The difference in the "Bad Boys" and a man of God is the "Bad Boys" have something wrong with their conscience. They do not care about your needs and desires. They lack ability to love or be loved. They also have an inability to abide by normal rules.

I have been there, seen that, done that and wrote a book about it. You made instant contact with the "Bad Boy" and you felt instant sparks almost like some invisible magnetic energy which draws you to each other. You feel a sense of passion or love at first sight. You may meet the sweet, attractive and successful man, but you do not feel attractive to him.

A man of God may seem boring and you may feel there is no passion or he is too nice. This passion you desire could very well be your concept of passion which really is your addiction to the wrong types of guys- "Bad Boys." Our minds can actually become addicted to emotional intensity and we move to an exhilarating high which feel like a roller coaster producing excitement.

Resist this temptation which attempts to keep you blinded. Once you are blinded, you do not see weakness, strengths, or pitfalls. If you have found yourself interested in "Bad Boys", stop seeking "Bad Boys" with warped values and negative behavior. Seek first the kingdom of God and His righteous and all those other things will be added.

You cannot squeeze lemon juice out of a grapefruit. Whatever is in the "Bad Boys will manifest. Therefore, stop looking for the "Bad Boys." If you let go of the wrong people, the right people will flow in. "You can be alright until Mr. Right comes along."

ARE YOU SLEEPING WITH THE ENEMY?

Today I hear more conversation about strongholds, witch craft, voodoo, generational curses, and sorcery. To break strongholds, you will need God to allow you to enjoy God's freedom. The question is: Are we committed to walk in the flesh or the spirit? We are in a spiritual battle which cannot be won in the flesh. When you embark upon a relationship and the man tries to consume you with activities of the flesh: petting, lust, and sex before marriage, please be aware. If your mate or acquaintance tries to encourage you to go against the will of God by lust, petting or having sex before marriage (fornication), you are attempting to or you are sleeping with the enemy.

Flee fornication. Every sin that a man doeth is without the body; but he that commiteth fornication sinneth against his own body. What? Know ye that your body is the temple of the Holy Ghost which is in you, which ye have of God, and ye are not your own? For ye are bought with a price: therefore glorify God in your body and in your spirit, which are God's. 1 Corinthians 6: 18-20.

Do not allow lust to overtake you. Lust is an insatiable spirit which arouses the flesh. What do you do when you get "holiness and freakiness?" Protect your "precious diamond." Once you give yourself over to lust, it has power to absolutely destroy you. Love gives and lust takes. Lust can become your god. Move away from the man who entices you into the lust cycle. He is definitely the enemy.

Flee youthful lusts: but follow righteousness, faith, charity, peace, with them that call on the Lord out of a pure heart. 2 Timothy 2:22.

By now I am sure you are saying. This God stuff is not fun. Ask yourself, how many male/female experiences in which you have slept with the enemy have been successful? Did this relationship manifest in connecting you to Mr. Right or Mr. Wrong?

Rev. Clarence Jackson, pastor of the Destiny Center, stated: "Ladies, if the only thing he is doing is sleeping with you, you are not his girlfriend or his boo. You are actually more like his mattress…"

Now concerning the things whereof ye wrote unto me: It is good for a man not to touch a woman. Nevertheless, to avoid fornication, let every man have his own wife, and let every woman have her own husband. 1 Corinthians 7:1-2

Many great men in the Bible experience a fallen state (Samson and David) which occurred due to the lust of the flesh, the lust of the eyes and the pride of life. You are encouraged to submit to God and the devil will flee from you. Remember these things become strongholds when our minds become contrary to the Words of God. Obedience is better than sacrifice. The enemy controls our behavior through our thoughts. As a man or woman thinks so is he or she. Do not let the enemy steal your joy. The joy of the Lord is your strength. "You can be alright until Mr. Right comes along."

Marriage is honorable in all, and the bed undefiled: whoremongers and adulterers God will judge. Hebrews 13:4

Sisters, remember man is conqueror and a warrior. John moves to Josephine and he conquers her. He now continues on to Sabrina and he conquers her. He later dates Alice and she is committed to God's commandment. John may leave her but he never forgets her; he thinks about her often and eventually tries to conquer her again and again. She becomes a challenge to him-someone he engages in a pursuit of. Sleeping with the enemy comes to rob and destroy your destiny.

Please do not be afraid of the enemy walking away from you. When he walks away from you, let him go. You cannot make a man stay if he wants to walk away. If he wants to stay nothing can keep him away. You have got to know when it is over. "You can be alright until Mr. Right comes along."

They that went out from us, but they were not of us; for if they had been of us, they would no doubt have continued with us: but they went out, that they might be made manifest that they were not of us.

For the weapons of our warfare are not carnal but mighty through God to the pulling down of strongholds. 2 Corinthians 10: 4

I CAN DO BAD ALL BY MYSELF

The Bible says if a man does not work, he shall not eat. Mr. Right should be someone who can enhance your life. He should be a man who can take you to the next level. If you are living in poverty, you should not hook up with a man and still do not have any food to eat.

Reverend Jamal Harrison Bryant says, "When she gets married, she ought to dress better, drive better, live better and eat better, not constantly in a struggle over where her next meal is coming from. My grandmother used to say, "I can do "bad" all by myself."

The woman who desires a man who can take her to another place should be a Proverbs 31 woman-virtuous woman. Her life is based on Proverbs 31:10-31. She is a wise woman who has taken the time to prepare household for good and not evil.

Who can find a virtuous woman? For her price is far above rubies. Proverbs 31: 10

Her husband and family count her priceless. She brings value to her family that cannot be measured. Her husband can trust his heart with her without fear of embarrassment and shame. She will do him "good" all the days of his life. She will not bring harm to him and want to see him be all the best he can be.

If you find yourself in a toxic relationship, you have to remember engaging in such a relationship is a sign of low self-esteem. Persons with low self-esteem feel worthless, unloved, incompetent, stupid and ugly. You can develop positive self-esteem by having good experiences with friends, neighbors in social settings, church, social clubs and other settings. When your self-esteem is high, you feel you can achieve because you know you are effective, lovable, capable, productive, important, and intelligent. If you enhance your self-esteem, you can definitely be alright until Mr. Right comes along. You do not have to remain in a negative toxic relationship. You can overcome because you are more than a conqueror with Christ

Jesus. Take it to a higher level! "You can be alright until Mr. Right comes along."

Nay, in all these things we are more than conquerors through him that loved us. Romans 8: 36

THE STRUGGLE CONTINUES

Do not leap into relationships too fast. And after we have been on three or more dates, we start trying out the man's last name. Let's not fantasize and end up making the wrong choice. Everything that glitters is not gold. Sometimes, we want a commitment so fast we begin to pressure the man about his intentions before the relationship has a chance to develop. "When will you buy the engagement ring?"

We deceive ourselves by making more out of what is actually going on in the relationship. "I know I am the one for John." He is Mr. Right and I am Ms. Right.

Sometimes, women suffer from the "I'll never-be-able-to-find-another man" syndrome. "I am thirty years of age. This has to be Mr. Right. Time is running out for me. I do not want to be 40 and single. I am watching my biological clock, and I want to have children before I am thirty."

Sisters make excuse for our mate's negative behavior. John is afraid of making a commitment because of his awful relationship with his father. Men can't be trusted; therefore, you got to treat them like a dog. We stay in bad relationships too long. "I will change Carl because I am a good woman."

In too many relationships, women center their lives too much on the relationship and not the individual fulfillment. "There is no need for me to go to college because Mr. Right has to make $150,000 a year and be able to take care of me."

Do you frequently have fantasies of love that is impossible? Women may fantasize about their father. I will marry Steve when he takes me on vacations like my dad did with my mom."

Do you try too hard to please a man? "Jeff is number one in my life and nothing will come before him. Life is nothing without a man to cuddle up to daily." We blame ourselves and feel guilty when things go wrong. "Omar decided to call it quits with me because of my big hips."

Are you blaming yourself because Mr. Right has not come along? "I am to blame for being so choosy. I would be married if I was not so choosy." At certain times we grab for any man. "I will settle for Jerome even though we are not the most compatible. I refuse to be lonely anymore."

He is not Mr. Right if you never meet any of his family or friends. Pay attention if he wants to spend time at your place but never invites you to his place. Check him out if when you go out it is always somewhere far away and not around your local places. You know you need to open your eyes if you never go out for dates and the excuse: "Baby, I just do not like being around people; I just like being around you." The struggle continues because you choose to continue to walk in darkness and not walk in the light. Do not be desperate but do be patient and wait on God to bless you.

What about revealing what your desires are. Do you expect a man to read your mind? "If he loves me, he would know what turns me on." He cannot read your mind. Let's not be too obsessed with love. "There is something wrong with me because men do not find me attractive. When will a man love me- at twenty, thirty, forty or fifty?" You can love at any age. "You can be alright until Mr. Right comes along."

This I say then, Walk in the Spirit, and ye shall not fulfill the lust of the flesh. For the flesh lusteth against the Spirit, and the Spirit against the flesh: and these are contrary the one to the other: so that we cannot do the things that ye would. But if ye be led by the Spirit, ye are not under the law. Now the works of the flesh is manifest, which are these; Adultery, fornication, uncleanness, lasciviousness, Idolatry, witchcraft, hatred, variance, emulations, wrath, strife, seditions, heresies, envyings, murders, drunkenness, revellings, and such like: of the which I tell you before, as I have also told you in time past, that they which do such things shall not inherit the kingdom of God. But the fruit of the spirit is love, joy, peace, longsuffering,

gentleness, goodness, faith, meekness, temperance: against such there is a law. And they that are Christ's have crucified the flesh with the affections and lusts. If we live in the Spirit, let us also walk in the Spirit. Galatians 5: 16-25

Deal With It

DEALING WITH TEMPTATIONS

Temptations will always be with you. We will be tempted by the devil. We will see couples which appear to be happily married. We will sometimes witness love affairs on TV, at the movies and yes even on Facebook which are quite tempting. Our friend will call us to talk about her new "boo". You may have a crush on the handsome man at your office. Sometimes, the boss will express an interest in you, and you see this can be an opportunity to advance on the job. You may be experiencing financial hardships and see the married man as a "sugar daddy." Please do not be deceived.

The thief cometh not, but to steal, and to kill, and to destroy: I am come that they might have life, and that they may have it more abundantly. John 10:10

The way to deal with temptations is to love God more than we love ourselves. This requires a woman to deny herself- to kill the flesh. The flesh is not good for nothing. If we do not wash the flesh, the flesh will smell a foul odor. If we do not take care of the flesh, the flesh will get sick. No matter what you do, the flesh will die.

Lust of the eyes, the lust of flesh and the pride of life cause death and destruction. When we are tempted and give in to our temptations, we may experience "temporary pseudo" happiness which seems like a "high." This is short lived which later reveal we have been set up for destruction. The married man told us that the only reason he stays with his wife is because of the children. He later revealed he would never consider divorcing his wife.

Temptations that often get men into negative behavior are the 3 G's: gold (money), girls (women and sex) and glory (pride). The 3 G's influence men in the world and men of God. What are your temptations?

But each one is tempted when, by his own evil desire, he is dragged ways and enticed. Then after desire has conceived, it gives birth to sin; and sin, when it is full grown, gives birth to death. James 1: 14-15

Submit yourself therefore to the God. Resist the devil and the devil will flee (James 4:7). With every temptation that comes your way, God will give you a way to escape.

There hath no temptation taken you but such as is common to man: but God is faithful, who will not suffer you to be tempted above that ye are able; but will with the temptation also make a way to escape, that ye may be able to bear it. 1 Cor. 10:13

Our conscience often directs us to examine ourselves. You may be thinking I am constantly reminded of fornication which I have engaged in for years. You may focus on the married man you are currently engaging in a relationship with. You may say I have sinned and I know God sees all that I do. I say we all fall short of the glory of God.

If we confess our sins, He is faithful and just to forgive us our sins, and to cleanse us from all unrighteousness. 1 John 1:9

In dealing with temptation, it is wise to anticipate the situation, formulate your natural response and to implement your prayerful planned response. Prayer is the key to unlock the binding hold temptation can have. No prayer- no power; little prayer- little power; and much prayer- much power.

We often make excuses just as Adam did in the beginning when he blamed eating from the forbidden tree on the woman God sent him. We often blame temptations and sin on our parents. There are times when some individuals get so confused that they get angry with God. Correct thinking is necessary for healing and delivery of temptations and sin.

When tempted, no one should say, God is tempting me. For God cannot be tempted by evil, nor does He tempt anyone. James 1:13.

Do not deceive yourself into believing based on faulty thinking. You may never get an opportunity to make love to this man again. He is too fine to resist. My body is yearning to get close to this fine, handsome, rich man. I have dreams about making love to this man every night.

Refrain from beating yourself up because you are tempted. It is not wrong to be tempted. Yielding to the temptation is the problem. So my question is: Is the situation the problem or how you respond to the situation? Is temptation the problem or how you respond to temptation?

To overcome temptation, make sure that your thought process is in line with the Word of God. Next, be open to hear the voice of the Lord. The Bible says "my sheep knows my voice." Hear from the Lord. God's voice is often a soft voice. The voice of the world often tries to drown out this soft voice of God with a loud voice. When God says no and show you the way out, hear and obey the voice of the Lord. Yes, obedience is better than sacrifice. If you do not obey God, you will sacrifice in one way or the other. You will sacrifice time, energy, money, and maybe your life.

Worship God daily thanking Him for the many blessings He has bestowed upon you. Thank God for all things: Thank you, God, for ending my relationship with the man I loved which was not good for me. God, I thank you that our relationship did not end in marriage. Thank you, God, that you gave me the spirit of discernment that I may see the game which was being played on me. God, I thank you that even though my marriage ended in divorce, I am blessed to nurture and raise my children. God, I thank you that I am single and given the opportunity to develop a personal and intimate relationship you.

For I am persuaded, that neither death, nor life, nor angels, nor principalities, nor powers, nor things present, nor things to come, Nor heights, nor depth, nor any other creature, shall be able to separate us from the love of God, which is in Christ Jesus our Lord. Romans 8:38

"You can be alright until Mr. Right comes along."

ARE YOU SCARING MEN OFF?

Sometimes, you may wonder why me Lord! I am a strong intelligent woman. I have worked hard to finish college and earned my doctorate degree. I love God and I am active in my church. I pay my tithes monthly. Yet Mr. Right has not crossed my path. Men leave me alone.

Why is it that so many women have so many positive attributes but are alone? Why is it that they may be able to hook a man but can't hold him? We may ask the question: What is wrong with men today? Women ask questions like do I need to lower my standards? Why do the women who appear to have street values get the good men? Do men appreciate women who are intelligent and accomplished? Why do I have difficulty getting a date?

We have to remember that skills that make us successful in the church, community or on the job are not the skills that make us successful in a relationship. Relationship building requires making decisions that not only gratify you but satisfy others. It means doing things that will keep the peace rather than achieve the goal. Sometimes, it may mean creating the peace in the first place.

I know this may sound like a mistake but in too many cases, when dealing with men, you will have to sacrifice being right in order to enjoy being loved. Being regarded as the head of household is especially important to men. This is especially important to black men, since their manhood is challenged everywhere else. Many modern women in today's society are so independent, committed to community causes, to the church, to their jobs that they project "I do not need a man" message. So they end up without a man in their life and often making the statement "I can do "bad" by myself."

A man may be interested but later began to feel that you do not have time for him. Achieving women have so many priorities that they place the man so low on their priority list, and the man's interest wanes or decreases.

Life becomes consumed with work, school, church and entertaining our girlfriends that we have little time for a man in our life.

Are you so busy with your concerns to listen to a man or to cook him a meal? Now this may surprise you. Soon the man will use the woman for only committed sex since she appears unavailable for anything else. Let's not miss the message. Let's not play into the problem by being blind thinking that "Men only want one thing." Faulty thinking moves the woman to decide she is better off with the degrees than the friendship. Could she one day wish she had set different priorities? We have to learn the skills to integrate our lives.

Scriptures cited in the Bible are for our inspiration. Yet, we have to be able to do more than recite scriptures. We have to be able to apply scriptures in our everyday living. It is more fruitful to be a sermon than to hear a scripture.

We have many societal ills today. The daily news reflect these ills which many women devote fighting spirits to do whatever they can for the glory of God and the good of the people. This is very good to help others but it must be kept in perspective. Do you want to save the world and lose your man? A fighting spirit is necessary on the battlefield but a kinder, gentler spirit is best for the home front.

Contemporary women downplay and sometimes forget their traditional feminine attributes. Believe me, men value women best for the ways they are different from them, not the ways they are the same. Men appreciate them for their grace and beauty-our feminine charm. Men enjoy our softness and see it as a way to be in touch with their tender side, a side they try not to show to other men. A hard working woman is great to have on your committee or team at work. But when a man comes "home sweet home" he prefers a loving partner to a hard worker.

Now it is not easy to make this transition for many women. It sounds submissive, oppressive, and outmoded. Women have had to fight for so many things. They have known so many men who are jive and untrustworthy. Let's face the truth. Many women are jive and untrustworthy also. Let's face the truth because the truth will set us free. Some women are set in their own ways. Not having a husband allows them to do whatever they want, when and how they want to do it. Having a husband means they have to share the power and in certain situations will have to surrender.

We are terrified of marriage and commitment. A friend of mind is "shacking up" with her male lover. I asked about her considering marriage. She told me she will never do that again. She is afraid of getting married but dreads the prospect of being single and alone.

Be not deceived; God is not mocked: for whatsoever a man soweth, that shall he also reap. For he that soweth to his flesh shall of the flesh reap corruption; but he that soweth to the Spirit shall of the Spirit reap life everlasting. Galatians 6: 7-8

Some sisters throw themselves into work to fill the void. But just like any other addiction, the escape often becomes the cage. How do we break the addiction? To make the break we need to do less and to "be" more. I am learning that Rome was not built in a day. I am learning that sometimes we can do so many good "things"; we miss what God has "best" for our lives. I am learning to let go and let God. I am learning to stop competing with men and to start collaborating with them.

A man who has been interest in me told me that "He gives me permission to be more aggressive with him." I of course said no to his request. I am learning to temper my assertive and aggressive energy with softness and serenity. I have come to realize that I and many of my smart and independent sisters are out of touch with our feminine center and therefore out of touch with our men.

Dancing today is quite different from forty years ago. Today, we get on the dance floor and express our creativity. We use to do a dance called the "two steps." I love this dance and it allowed me to follow the man's lead. I did not feel inferior because his part was different from my part. I did not feel I had to prove that I was as capable to lead as he was. I simply allowed him to take my hand, and I would go with the flow. Yes, we can learn how to bring some of that spirit and skills to our relationship. Can we learn how to accept his lead and go with the flow? We must remember that he has to demonstrate leadership skills first. We are in an advantageous position when we recognized that God made man to be His glory and woman to be the glory of man. Who is leading whom? "You can be alright until Mr. Right comes along."

WHY SOME WOMEN SETTLE FOR MAN-SHARING?

I have heard some women say that a piece- of- man is better than no man at all. Can you imagine a woman who settles for a piece man? Some of these women willingly share someone else man. If you are fully aware of the committed relationship and agree to an outside relationship, you are engaging in man sharing.

These women are referred to as home wreckers who rather spend their days and nights with someone else man than find their own. This is how they spend their time not even attempting to wait on Mr. Right. They brag about the fun they have and that when she is not with her man for the moment, she is strolling around in the finest clothes, getting weekly manicures and pedicures, taking cruises and enjoying the finer things of life, using his bank account or credit cards. To most women the man sharer is perceived as the enemy.

Let put man sharers in the proper prospective. Some man sharers are pillars in the community and some are elders in the church. Some of these sisters are holding on to the dream that one day he will be theirs and no one else. Some man sharers are married themselves. These women want to get their needs met and these needs can be emotional, physical, the need for companionship or a financial need. Some women man share just for sex.

There is a shortage of African American men which has encouraged or forced some women to man share. Many women in committed relationships are sharing their man unbeknown to them. They settle because society says they should have a man and not be alone. They believe it is not fashionable to be alone. These women believe there is something wrong with you if you are alone. On the flip side the man sharer is more likely to be lonely in heart.

Think about Nina Simone's song, "Other Woman." "The lonely woman will always cry herself to sleep...the other woman will never have his love to keep…and as the years go by, the other woman will spend her life alone." What about Beyoncé's song, "if you like it put a ring on it." In essence, let's get married.

I believe a woman who willingly shares a man is afraid of commitment. There are issues in her life. She may have observed her father cheat on her dear mother. She may have experienced abuse in her life. She constantly feels depress when she is alone. Man sharers should remember all good things come to an end sooner or later.

Man sharers need to get the message to get their own stuff. They do not have to share a man with another woman. One principle I try to live by is not to date any woman's man and definitely not date another woman's husband. God spoke to me one day to live by this principle because I may have to pray for this sister. One day, I attended Church where a sister was in love with the visiting minister who had expressed an interest in me. The minister of this church asked an evangelist to come up and pray for two other ministers whom she had called to the front of the church. I said to myself. "Good, she has her minister to pray." Would you believe this minister called me out also to pray? I said to myself. "Obedience is better than sacrifice." So I went to the front of the church and prayed as requested. When I open my eyes, the sister who was also interested in the visiting minister that I was interested in was at the front of the church also for me to pray for her.

I got a confirmation on what God told me: Not to date a woman's man or woman's husband. This may mean I will often be alone but I am convinced God knows what is best for me. I choose to listen and obey God.

There is a way that seemeth right to man, but the end thereof are the ways of death. Proverbs 16:25.

Men know there is always a woman out there who will cheat with them. I know man sharers have their goal in mind. However, when man sharing is exposed, wives, husbands, the other women and yes the game players get hurt. Do not be deceived. What you need to know is if a man wants to mess around, he is going to keep approaching women until he finds the one who will play. After all he is a warrior and a conqueror- that what he is and what he does. If you give him a little opening, he will take it. You let a man know you are willing to go there when you entertain his conversation or take his credit card.

A man knows not to try and take you there if you make it clear that you are not willing to play. Ask the magic question: Are you seeing someone at this time? If he lets you know he is married or he is kicking it with someone else, then do not be shy and let him know that you have no interest in kicking it with a man who is already in a relationship. I assure you he will move on. In the meantime, you will be ready and available for someone who wants to be involved solely with you. Remember, all your gifts have your name written on them. "You can be alright until Mr. Right comes along."

If You knew Better-
You Would Do Better

YOU DO NOT HAVE TO SETTLE-YOU ARE BETTER THAN ABUSE

Too many women today feel that they have to settle to have a man in their life. Many women feel that a "piece of a man" is better than no man at all. God says He can provide everything you need.

Therefore, you do not have to allow abusive relationships control you. You are better than abuse. Abusive relationships are too common today. I see abusive relationships play out on television and on the local and national news.

Please do not settle. If you experience someone kicking you, hitting you, choking you, biting you, punching you, bruising you, forcing you to do something against your will, frequently insulting you or threatening you with violence, you are being abused. I hope you see the "red flag." Get out in a hurry. Trust me, sister, God has something better in store for you.

You do not want to allow abusive relationships to block your blessings. Abusive relationships can cause you to feel shame, fear, embarrassment, anger, guilt and helplessness.

You are better than that. The feelings experienced by abusive relationships often prohibit you from taking actions. Sometimes, victims feel responsible and blame themselves for what happens to them. This abusive relationship is not love but control motivated by fear.

There are approximately six million American women who are beaten each year by their husbands or boyfriends. Approximately 4000 of them are killed. A relationship should enhance your life-not destroy your life.

You are too precious to be abuse. Love the one you are with. Again I say be willing to be with you until the right one shows up. "You can be alright until Mr. Right comes along."

WHAT'S LOVE GOT TO DO WITH IT?

When I was a young girl attending Sunday school, we use to discuss love. I remember learning at an early age the powerful word of love. Our Sunday school teacher would ask: "Who is God?" We were taught: God is love. Therefore, God equals love. Another question which was asked: "Where is God?" We were taught God is everywhere. Well, if God is love and love is everything, then God intends for love to be everywhere- church, family, community, and relationships throughout the state, nation and the world.

We do not want to sing the song that Tina Turner sings: "What's love got to do with it?" Let us not get confused. God is not the author of confusion. Wherever there is confusion, God is not in the midst of it. God is love. God says there are three important virtues: love, faith and hope and the greatest of all is love.

Charity (Love) is long suffering and kind. Love is not jealous, it does not brag, does not get puffed up, does not behave indecently, does not look for its own interest, and does not become provoked. Love does not rejoice over unrighteousness, but rejoice with truth. It bears all things, believes all things, and endures all things. Love never fails. 1 Corinthians 13:4-8

It is heavy when we think of God's love. Have you ever thought about how much God loves you? He loves us so much that He gave his only begotten son, Jesus Christ. Tell yourself "God loves me." Stand in front of the mirror and tell yourself again "God loves me. " Tell your sister or brother "God loves you, too."

Everyone wants love but many fear love. There are two prevailing emotions. Whatever we do, we do because of love or fear. God says He did not give us the spirit of fear. He says He gave us the power of Love and a sound mind.

There is confusion today about what love is. If there is confusion about love, there is confusion about who God is. If there is confusion about who

God is, then the devil is having his way. The devil is on his job: to rob, steal and destroy. The devil is busy 24 hours a day-7days a week.

What is love? Many individuals have a problem defining love. Some say love is a feeling or emotions. Some say what I use to say when I was in the third grade: Love is an itching of the heart that you can't scratch. I say love is more than a feeling or an emotion. I say love is compassion coupled with action and it often requires a sacrifice. Many people are afraid to make a sacrifice so they psyche themselves out to believe love is a feeling.

Love is often based on many things. To some love is based on physical attraction. I have heard ladies say they like the way 50 Cent looks. They say "he is so handsome." They say they would like to have his baby even though they have never had a conversation with him. They want to have his baby but never say they truly love 50 Cent. The Bible shows that, to be of true value, love must go beyond affection or mutual attraction, and be governed by what is the highest good for our brothers and sisters. What does love have to do with it?" We need love. We need God!

God says if we love Him we will obey Him. Do you love God enough to obey his commandments? Partial obedience is not obedience. Do you love God enough to trust Him to send Mr. Right in your life? We ought to love God enough to please Him. We should try to live according to God's purpose and not man's purpose. Remember love gives and lust takes. "You can be alright until Mr. Right comes along."

DO YOU WANT REAL SINCERE LOVE?

I want you to know, these days, Mr. Right is truly in demand. Mr. Right clearly understands this fact. There are not enough Mr. Rights to go around and too few desiring to make a commitment. What is the portrait of Mr. Right? To many women, Mr. Right has the right diploma, right job, drives the right car and wears the right designer label.

Women are advised that they should not be unequally yoked. Yet too often, they overlook the most important qualities because they take the right road making the wrong turn. They too frequently overlook brothers who do not appear to fit into the book that they believe will produce love, happiness and security. Take another look! A man's appearance is not everything and you can't judge the book by looking at the cover.

And ye shall know the truth, and the truth shall make you free. John 8: 32

A young sister told me how she had met a young man who scrubbed toilets and mopped floors as a maintenance man. He only had a GED certificate but he was a very nice guy. She said she initially wondered what they had in common. What surprised her was when she started to feel the strength of his love. She informed me that she is now so glad that she did not close off dating someone just because he did not have a glamorous job. She now has someone she loves and someone who is handy around the house.

Love is patient. It does not envy, it is not proud. It is not rude, it is not self-seeking, it is not easily angered, it keeps no records of wrong. Love does not delight in evil but rejoices with the truth. It always protects, always trusts, always hopes, always perseveres. Love never fails… And now three remain: faith, hope, love. But the greatest of these is love. 1 Corinthians 13: 4-8, 13 (NIV)

A medical doctor may have a big bank account. However, the bus driver or the Fed Ex guy may not have some of the qualities on your list, but he may possess character. He may possess the ability to fulfill your yearning heart.

It is time to stop reflecting on what a man has and where he works and become mindful of who this man is and what he actually has to offer. Questions to answer are: Is he honest? Is he kind? Does he love God? Does he love you? There are really brothers out there who are single, available and ready to love you. It is actually possible to find a deeply committed relationship that honors you. Despite what you have heard, winning in a love affair is not about identifying the right circle of men or knowing how to play the game. It is necessary to examine our preconceived notions about ourselves, men and dating.

The truth is most women, at some point in life will be led to examine their beliefs and self-defeating approaches to finding true love. You may find your way to love when you change your thinking, let go of attitudes that make you settle for less than you hope for, dream for and so much deserve. Let's try seeing men we meet in a whole new way. We have to teach our daughters how to distinguish between a man who lusts after her and a man who loves her. "You can be alright until Mr. Right comes along."

DOES HE REALLY LOVE ME?

You find yourself happy and then you are sad, depending on what love ball he throws your way. The more you give of yourself to make him love you, the less he gives. The less he gives, the more desperate you become.

Your mind gets confused and you begin to have dialogue with yourself or your best friend. He is probably leading me on. If he returns your love but only a little bit, he gives just enough to keep you hooked on him. He does not tell you to get out of his life, but he never quite returns your love all the way either. He is probably leading you on if he says things like "I love you, but I do not want to get involved right now." He is probably leading you on and he wants to keep you on edge guessing.

Does this sound like you? If you answer yes, you may have a fatal attraction to the wrong men. You will probably meet hundreds of men in your life time. You do not have to choose ready- made losers if you can spot them ahead of time.

No woman can honestly judge another. Almost every woman gets involved with at least one Mr. Wrong in her life. She may marry him, live with him or just "go" with him. Women who get involved with the wrong man have one thing in common-they all say they did not know he was like that. He was so nice in the beginning. She was definitely in the "sparkle" stage of the relationship. She later says "How was I to know?" They are always charming in the beginning. You are so impressed with the "good" side that you begin to put up with the bad side.

While you are waiting on Mr. Right, you can spare yourself a lot of headaches if you know who these creeps are-Mr. Wrong.

The Bag Man: Does He Really Love Me?

The Bag Man is easy to recognize because he arrives at your house and just stay- bags and all. He does not have to call home because he does not have one. He always has enough clothes to last for about one month.

His clothes, dog and cat are in the car and so is most of what he owns. He always arrives at your home broke and hungry. When he gets to your house, he will stay as long as you feed him and give him plenty of love. He is handsome and sweet and a great lover. He has a way of fitting in. He may tell you he has either made a fortune or has just lost one. He expects you to "mother" him until he makes his next fortune. I do not care how much you give the Bag Man he does not give anything back, except for playing the saxophone and making passionate love. He may become romantic and play a song made and dedicated especially for you. You can easily get rid of the Bag Man by cutting off his support system- asking him for rent or money to buy grocery. I now hear him singing James Brown's song, "Papa got a brand new bag."

The Ticking Time Bomb: Does He Really Love Me?

The Ticking Time Bomb comes with much junk in his trunk -compulsive gambler, drug abuser, wife abuser, smooth alcoholic and just plain crazy waiting to explode. You see his outside but if you could see his inside or inner person, you would not go near him. He is also attractive and charming on the surface, and it is difficult to hear the ticking hidden explosive he carries around daily. He has an unstable personality under the handsome veneer. He is so nice in the beginning and because you do not see him completely, you get hooked. Just as you think true love has come your way and this is definitely Mr. Right, an explosion rocks your world. At first, you do not recognize that his behavior is a pattern. He may tell you that he has been reformed and he does not cheat anymore. He runs away with your best friend when you are five months pregnant. He expects you to still stay with him-loving him. I hear tick -tock –tick-tock about to explode. You better get out of the way!

The Judge: Does He Really Love Me?

The judge speaks from his own perfection. His mind tells him he has it going on. He rarely works preferring to tell other people what to do and how to do it. When you meet him, he gives you his credentials and credits and tries to impress you how blessed you are that he has chosen you. He knows the game and he plays you like he is playing chess. He will tell you how to dress, how to wear your hair, how to handle your job, even what you want in love making. As long as you agree with him you can get along with him and he is happy. He knows what you need the most is him. Life is real and there are moments when things go sour in the relationship. This is when he starts to judge you and tear your self-confidence in pieces. Defiance is the best way to get rid of the judge. Make plans with your friends whom he does not like. Wear the green dress with the split on the side which he told you not to wear again. Do things the opposite of what he told you not to and he will flee.

Double Minded: Does He Really Love Me?

The double- minded man has difficulty making a decision. He is not sure of anything including whether or not he wants to be with you. One reason he is not able to make up his mind is because he is greedy. He wants it all. Every second he is with you, he believes he is missing out on something. He is on a chase and he never quits looking even after he is married. The double- minded man is never happy or satisfied. The double minded man changes his position in a moment. He decides to change his career, home, friends, and where he will lives. His mind is wandering a large portion of the time. The double- minded man needs to be counseled by a professional-not in a relationship with you. A double- minded man has steak life style with a hamburger mentality. He is a two timed loser. A double minded person is unstable in all of his ways.

The Mother's Patient: Does He Really Love Me?

The mother's patient really wants you to take care of him. His mother was not very warm and loving and he is still looking for the woman who will make up for his mother's inadequacies. He yearns for your motherly instinct. He desires that you be sympathetic toward him. Mother's patient has been known to fake illness so that he can be taken care of. You can get rid of the mother's patient by letting him know that you do not have any medication in the house, and he will have to heal himself through faith healing. This is a mommy boy looking for a lover in pursuit of his mother.

The Wheeler Dealer: Does He Really Love Me?

The wheeler dealer has a fascination with ill-gotten gains and has a fear of working. He has deal making appeal. He takes pride in making a deal. He will even offer you a profit. All you have to do is go out with three of his buddies, and he will take you on stolen credit card shopping spree. If you go out with him, it will get worse. Soon he will treat you like he is "pimping" you as his mistress. The best way to get rid of him is to tell him that you think the policemen are watching your house. Be aware that the Wheeler Dealer will trick you, and the next thing you know you are on the street to be pimped by the player-the Wheeler Dealer.

The Divorced Junkie: Does He Really Love Me?

The divorced junkie has recently divorced and appears to be an emotional basket case that does not have healthy emotions, personality or commitment. He may get better after a year or more. The question is do you want to be the first woman he gets involved with after his divorce? The divorced junkie is hurting, bleeding and too involved with his own pain and losses to make a good mate for you. The way to deal with the divorced junkie is to refuse to listen to any more of his stories about his ex-wife, his divorce, child support, what he lost, his kids or his past. He uses divorce as his crutch and his excuse.

Married Never Again: Does He Really Love Me?

He has been married too many times and he did not like it. He does not believe in some of life occurrences-making money, ironing clothing, eating meat, woman wearing make-up, or watching television. When you first meet him, he is so charming and disarming about his easy ways. This man knows your inner soul and appears to show much love. He makes eye contact and he appears to see your inner soul. Once he sees that you are comfortable with him and agree to turn over your possessions (car, money and credit card) to him, he flips the script and begins question why are you with him? He is determined to never make a commitment or get married again. The best way to deal with the Married Never Again is refuse to iron his favorite white shirt and do not open the door the next time he knocks.

The Savior: Does He Really Love Me?

The savior is the type who is almost impossible to resist. He is here to help you and he is not like those other men who were not so nice to you. He is different and will show you what real love is. Whatever your secret fantasy or desire is, the savior will provide. He will always make you happy, so he pretends to be whatever you have always wanted. He promises to make your dreams come true and is here to give you what you want and need. He is determined to convey to you that he loves you and he has wonderful things scheduled for you for the rest of your life. Yet when you most need him, he is nowhere to be found. Watch your caller ID to avoid his next call. He is not your savior because he is the real pretender. God is our only Savior.

The Lone Ranger: Does He Really Love Me?

He describes himself as "a bit of a loner." The lone ranger opens up what appears to be his heart. He is not an island unto himself and may wish to un-lone himself by being with you. The lone ranger can trick you because it is necessary to distinguish between the person who stands alone because he is independent and the man who stands alone because he can't get along with other people. The lone ranger expects you to open up and share but he keeps the doors in his life closed and locked. He demands to know what is happening in your world but behaves negatively if you ask about what is happening in his life when you are apart. The lone ranger has no friends and has little time for your friends. The lone ranger progresses through life refusing to get involved. Ultimately, he moves from being the lone ranger to a boring lone ranger with nothing to spice up life.

The Over Achiever: Does He Really Love Me?

The over achiever is usually married to a higher cause and dedicated to something higher than he. The over achiever is admired by society but is a lousy partner in a relationship. He pays little attention to you and is often too exhausted to do anything but sleep when he takes time off. He places little priority on your male/female love relationship and focuses most of his time on his passion. On a positive note, he is dependable but do not count on him having leisure time to spend with you. He is actually the man your mother dreamed of you marrying. You will most likely consider marrying him because he is financially secure and needs to be married so you think. If you try to get the over achiever away from his work, he will try to make you feel guilty. He is admired by many people but he is incapable of returning love. I hope you see the red flag because if you become the wife of the over achiever, you will spend your time as a lonely wife.

The Royal King: Does He Really Love Me?

The royal king's ego mission becomes to turn the more accomplished woman into a status-improver. He challenges a woman to make it her grand job of restyling him. His mission involves encouraging the woman to visit tailors for his clothes and upscale stores to purchase his shoes. He spends much of his time investing in his own interest or whatever you have to offer. He wants to receive the benefit package you can provide. The royal king is interested in self-improvement and his need for masculine superiority until a conflict takes place and he no longer wants to be taught, groomed and corrected. The royal king gets the top prize which is to absorb his classy girlfriend's success and status and later declare them as his own. He brags about his ladies career, house, car, and associates. Inwardly, he resents her achievements because they represent a threat to his own standing. He may boast about his lady's book to all his friends implying that her success was due largely to him. "The royal king is something else."

The Drama King: Does He Really Love Me?

The drama king knows the right things to say but nothing ever materializes that he says. In essence, he talks the talk but does not walk the walk. I know you have heard the true saying: "Action speaks louder than words." He will call your phone 50 times a day because he wants you to think of him every second of the day. He is so selfish that he does not want your life to be about anything or anyone but him. Therefore, he creates illusions in his head that you are with another man. He is so insecure that he daily creates some new dramatic situation. He is the drama king and he wants to be with you 24-7 because he fears you will leave him. He recognizes you as his special lady today but in a few days, you are no longer together. He says it is over and the next few hours he is calling you again and again. He has control issues, abandonment issues and issues of insecurity. He is a true drama king. You have to properly reason it in your mind. He can imagine in his mind that he is a king but please choose not to have this drama in your life.

Trust in the Lord with all thine heart; and lean not unto thine understanding. In all thy ways acknowledge him, and he shall direct thy paths. Proverbs 3: 5-6

It is to your advantage to recognize personal qualities and character in men. Give yourself time. Do not rush into a relationship. If he tries to rush you, most likely he is trying to hide something. Do not sign the contract without reading the fine print. It is alright if you read the fine print twelve or twenty times if this is what you feel. Obviously, you have some serious doubt. Take time to get to know him.

Watch, fight in the spirit and pray daily. Watch those individuals who always want to receive but rarely gives. Our ability to give and receive is necessary for a healthy relationship. This is called reciprocity. Unfortunately because of fear, many individuals spend countless hours trying to control so they can receive more than they are required to give. They will come to your house three times a week for dinner but forget your birthday and Valentine's day.

We have to examine ourselves and look at the reality as to whether the man we are interested in is capable of loving us. We have to ask some real important questions: Is he a mature or immature man? Are my expectations of this man realistic or unrealistic? Is he healthy emotional or is he emotional bankrupt? Is he capable of making a commitment? Does he operate daily in the real world or a world of fantasy? Is he wired up to love me the way I want to be loved? Does he want to embrace mature or subordinate women?

It is imperative to get to a place where you recognize that God is your source. When man leaves you, remember God will never leave you or forsake you. God can be a mother to the motherless and a father to the fatherless. He can be a lover to those who do not feel loved. God is love. Trust God all the way.

You can give without loving but you cannot love without giving. Remember love is more than a feeling or emotions. Love is as love does. Love is compassion coupled with action, and it often requires a sacrifice. "You can be alright until Mr. Right comes along."

COMPUTER LOVE

There is an increase in women and men who are meeting on-line. More and more people are joining Facebook. Facebook is fun, fast and convenient but be wise as a serpent and humble as a dove. Sometimes individuals joining Facebook are not really honest, and this can really ruin romance.

I met this guy on Facebook who appeared to be very handsome and charming. He moved very fast in the relationship by sharing with me that he was in the army and would soon be released from the army. He said the magic words: "I love you." He began to romance me on Facebook and later he requested that I get a yahoo account. Upon his release, he said he would be going to Africa to pursue his business venture. It turns out his business was buying gold.

He would arrange a daily dates with me on yahoo.com. To my surprise, he got caught up in Africa. He told me he would daily go to the gold mine in Africa to acquire gold to meet his goal. He later began to talk about meeting me when he comes back to the USA. He shared that he wants to make a commitment to me and later marry. Sound promising!

About two months into this computer relationship, he shared with me that he had run into a problem. He had the gold and his airfare but he did not have enough money to pay for his hotel or money to ship the gold from Africa to the USA. He asked me for money and he later began to put pressure on me. I let him know that I did not have money to send him and I ended our computer relationship.

Computer love is risky and can be dangerous. Some individuals have had success, but I encourage you to slow the process down. Do not assume you have made a homerun. Take time to check out the first, second, third and fourth base.

Ask yourself are all your Facebook friends truly your friends? Make sure you initially meet anyone introduced to you via computer in a public place. Tell a family member or friend where you will be and who you will be with. Never reveal everything about you, as you engage in the social media. If you are going to the Bahamas, do not put this out there in the social media. This is for your protection and security. You would not want to return home and your house has been broken into.

Be careful what you put out there in the social media. Think about this. Once this information is out there in the social media, it remains there. You may think you have erased this information. You may have forgotten about this specific information but it still remains there to be traced and investigated if necessary.

I know you may feel you have met someone special but please be aware. No sexting please! Sexting and revealing your body to the one you are infatuated with is illegal. Do not take a picture in the nude and send it via your cell phone even when he begs you to send it. He may even tell you he loves you. I say do not do it.

And be not conformed unto this world; but be ye transformed by the renewing of your mind, that ye may prove what is that good, and acceptable, and perfect will of God. Romans 12: 2

The last thing we need in a relationship is another reason to feel mistrust. Spending time on Facebook and other social networking sites can also foster jealousy especially when you look on the Facebook page of the guy you are interested in.

There are several dating sites online to choose from. Move with caution. Remember you have not met this individual. Take time to get to know him. Use good judgment in meeting him. If you meet him, try meeting in a private location where you feel safe. Trust your instincts and if you have a "check" in your spirit, take time to check it out. Have a little talk with Jesus. You can talk with God and Jesus about anything. This is what it means to have a personal and intimate relationship with God.

I know there are individuals who meet online and have developed successful relationships and marriages. I am not being totally negative. Be wise as a serpent and humble as a dove. Ask yourself are all of the friends that I meet online truly your friends? Ask yourself, do I trust all my online friends? Ask yourself, do I really know all my online friends? Ask yourself will I be comfortable going on a date with online friends?

You have to remember that computer love places you in a situation to social network with people all over the world. This is an adventure in itself to connect with people from different locations and different cultures. I know there are success stories out there where computer love has and is working. The challenge is to see the real man in the mirror. "You can be alright until Mr. Right comes along."

Got Hurt: Now Pull Yourself Together

IT DID NOT WORK AND I AM HURT

God has blessed me to know many women. I have had the opportunity to talk with many women who had or are currently experiencing pain, resulting from disappointing relationships. This hurt leaves some feeling like they never want to be in relationship with a man again. Some women are bitter and express that they dislike men and have turned to a female lover. Some women grow cold and feel they will play the game with the man and hurt men before they are hurt. Some women feel they are afraid to fall in love because they do not want to be hurt again.

Believe it or not, there is a select group of women who have experienced pain and made a decision to heal and go on with their lives, engaging in wholesome activities. No matter what hurt you have experienced God can take your pain and turn into a passion for the glory of God and the good of His people. Yes, you still have choices to make even when you have been hurt.

Brethren, I count not myself to have apprehended: but this one thing I do, forgetting those things which are behind, and reaching forth unto those things which are before, I press toward the mark for the prize of the high calling of God in Christ Jesus. Philippians 3:13-14

It is great therapy to learn how to forgive. Forgiveness is more for you than for the one who hurt you. Forgiveness is a process we go through which allows us to accept another individual- for not who we want him to be but for who he is.

Once I was hurt very bad from a relationship. My hurt was so painful that I felt that my body had been split into two halves and the community walked around viewing my blood trying to decide what was my blood type? The big question from many was could I survive this painful attack motivated by the enemy? Will she survive this weapon which has been formed against her? Where is her strength now? Who will comfort her tonight when she is alone or lonely?

"Let me tell you my God is able!" God is an awesome God! He is able to do exceedingly above anything you can think, dream or imagine. God is the way and He will see you through your hurt and pain. As a matter of fact, God will not put any more on you than you can bear. God will give you the grace to make it through day after day without destroying your mind. I know you may say I have been hurt so many times in the past. I feel what you are saying. When you think of the many times you have been hurt, it becomes easy to think about giving up. I don't care if you have been hurt a hundred times, do not give up. Keep getting up and keep looking up. If you can look up, you can get up. God is on your side and He will not let you fall.

For a just man falleth, seven times and riseth up again: but the wicked shall fall in mischief. Proverbs 24:16

Never dwell on the past whether you are experiencing victories or defeats. Every knock down is not a knock out. The battle is not over. You will be at battle with the devil until the day you die. The devil will not retreat from you until he causes you to abort the destiny God has for your life. You can defeat the devil where he tries to possess you with strongholds because with God we are more than a conqueror. It is not over until God says it is over!

Serena Williams made an announcement that she was in the process of swearing off dating because it was not working. Serena confessed to Celebuzz. She stated, "I have given up on dating. I am a really emotional person. I give my all and everything. I do make mistakes- like every human does- but the last relationship just was too much of a heart break for me. I just can't go through that anymore. It was hard."

You can turn pain into power; you can turn power into promise; you can turn promise into praise and you can turn praise into gain. You may feel like you failed. To fail is the first attempt in learning. Pain gives you instruction to pay attention inward now. Own your own pain. Until you pay attention to the wounds which dwells inside of you, you will continue to bleed, hurt and infections will occur. Owning your pain and paying attention to you and your pain allow you to start your healing process.

Do not mask the pain. This sometimes manifest in addictions used to mask pain- drug addiction, sex addiction, gambling addiction. In order to heal, deal with your pain. If he ran off with your best friend, I know you are in pain and hurting. In order to heal the pain, feel the pain, deal with the pain and allow God to heal the pain.

It is sometimes necessary to forgive yourself and to forgive others who may have hurt you. Let the past stay in the past. God did not place your eyes in the back of your head. He placed your eyes in the front of your head so you can look forward not backward. Learn from your past mistakes but be encouraged that you have the personal power to overcome them- with God. Do not allow others to control you by being bound to past hurt. You do not want to walk around daily with a heavy chain of un-forgiveness around your neck.

I know it is hard when you leave someone you love or someone you love leaves you. I know this is painful. I know you feel as though your body has been cut open and the pain lingers and the public walks around you to see how you will survive. You may feel like you are a loser because you have invested five or ten years into the relationship. You find yourself staying in in the relationship even though you fight every day. You stay in the relationship even though you don't like this person. You may have even grown apart. Believe me sometimes the break up is a blessing. Pull yourself together and look forward to the abundant life God promised you. "You can be alright until Mr. Right comes along."

SANCTIFIED, NOT SATISFIED AND STILL HURTING

Pain is a natural part of life. We will all experience pain- single people, married people, employed people, unemployed people, beautiful people, people who are aesthetical challenged, Black people, White people, male and females. We cannot avoid pain. God uses man's rejection to propel you in God's direction.

Reading the Bible enhances our relationship with God and increases our faith. Yet too many women interpret God's word in ways that leave them as victims hurting daily. In my role as an ordained minister and counselor, I have heard many women express why they cannot walk away from toxic relationships even when they are hurting and devaluing themselves as human beings.

I hear women who are suffering and making giant sacrifices endure for love and relationships. In essence, I hear women of God make excuses for their pain and suffering. "God is trying to teach me something." "Through all my suffering, I know God has something good in store for me." "God does not put you through no more than you can bear." "What does not hurt you will make you strong." "Weeping may endure for a night but joy cometh in the morning." "No cross no crown" "No guts no glory." "No pain no gain." Thinking God's thoughts can be helpful in shaping our mindset to understand that God is the way to our healing.

Women are expected to sometimes be too strong. We are taught that a good woman makes sacrifices even when she hurts because of constant pain. We have watched our mothers and grandmothers make great sacrifices to put food on the tables and many times to keep our sons alive. I see many women today suffer to support their families when men walk away.

Yes, we know God will make a way. Yet our hurting will not stop if we do not play our part. We can make sacrifices and be humble. To humble does not mean we think less of ourselves, we just think of ourselves less. We can deny ourselves (being selfless) but never forget to love ourselves. Putting other's desire before our desire does not mean we have to allow others to victimize us like we have no feelings.

When it comes to our man and our relationship, God does not expect us to give ourselves completely away in a relationship. It behooves us to save some self for yourself because you may need yourself one day.

You are not expected to stay in an abusive relationship where a man beats you, kicks you, spits on you and treats you like you are nothing but the scum of the earth. Leaving an abusive relationship does not indicate that you do not love and believe in God. You have to know when enough is enough. God commands us to love our neighbors as we love ourselves. There is nothing wrong with loving y-o-u. If you do not love yourself, you give others very little to love. Do get it twisted!

Sanctification is a process which sets an individual aside. The anointing comes often via hurt. Just because you are sanctified does not erase the pain. The church must be aware that the world is full of hurting people- many are sanctified. Many individuals who are hurting are experiencing shame, doubt or fear and many will not attend church. What often happens is that they spend years in the back of the pews trying to pay for something they did in the past.

The Bible never camouflaged the weakness of people. We all fall short of the glory of God. God used David. God used Abraham and his wife Sarah. Would you believe God used Rehab, the Jericho prostitute? We must change our mindset about wounded people.

Many hurt people feel they have fallen and cannot get up. They are broken and wounded people. The church must become the hospital to treat wounded people. The church is the hospital for wounded souls. The staff in the hospital understands that periodically people get sick and they need to recover. Jesus focused on hurting people.

When does love exceed hurt? How much do we have to hurt in the name of love? It is okay to love you. God wants you to love you. God does not want you to be broken, busted and disgusted. He came that you might have life more abundantly- more abundance in love, joy, peace, hope and all that is good. Despite what you feel, you do not have to be a sanctified victim hurting with pain. "You can be alright until Mr. Right comes along."

Forasmuch then as Christ hath suffered for us in the flesh, arm yourselves likewise with the same mind: for he that hath suffered in the flesh hath ceased from sin; That he no longer should live the rest of his time in the flesh to the lusts of men, but to the will of God. 1 Peter 4: 1-2

HE HURT ME AND I AM ANGRY

Yes, you thought he was Mr. Right, and you are hurt and very disappointed. You feel like you want to scream. Not only are you hurt-you are angry. You wonder how to handle this anger because you do not want to lose your cool or get ill. To better handle your emotions, it is wise to learn the source of your anger.

The key to understanding the rage that lies within, often subconscious, is to become aware of the great difference between realistic and unrealistic rage. Rage is defined as a violent outburst of rage in which self-control is lost. Realistic rage is justified rage that emerges naturally each time we feel threatened by someone who is a part of our reality. Unrealistic rage, on the other hand, arises from memories and fantasies of wish for revenge from childhood.

We all experience hurt and disappointment at some time in our lives. You have a personal choice about how you react to life's experiences. You may deal with anger in the following ways:

- Explosion. This expression of anger is emotion in motion. He is angry and he breaks your car window. Explosive behavior reflects internal anger. Some people explode and let their anger pass. How do you feel after you have exploded? Do you think you should have exploded? If you think you should not have done that, then you need to find a healthier way to express anger.
- Repression. Repressed anger is unexpressed anger. Some people can internalize anger so well that they fool others that they are not angry. Repressed anger can cause health problems like hypertension, stroke and heart disease. Several medical doctors I know have indicated this to be a fact.
- Suppression. With suppression, the person knows what she is feeling but chooses to withhold her emotions. You stuff your anger and do not want to discuss what is bothering you. Actually this creates a separation between you and the person you are angry with. If you should happen to feel distance from someone you care

about, you are suppressing your emotions. You make a decision to shut the person who hurt you out of your life. You avoid this individual.

- • Depression. Many cases of depression are caused by a biochemical imbalance. Depression reflects external anger. Other cases of depression are caused by an expression of repressed rage. Bottling up this powerful emotion can result in some people withdrawing and losing interest in others and in activities which are common signs of depression.

Most times anger stems from how we feel about ourselves. Johnny has been unfaithful to you. You become anger when there is a gap between what you feel you should be and what you believe you are. Beneath the anger there is pain- the pain of rejection, the pain of abandonment, the pain of loneliness. We often overlook another emotion which is the love of self. Only by working through the anger can you come to a place of truly knowing and loving yourself.

Be ye angry, and sin not; let not the sun go down upon your wrath; Neither give place to the devil. Ephesians 4: 26-27

You are anger at Johnny because he cheated on you. The first step is to tell you the truth. Start with a simple statement like "I am angry at Johnny because he cheated on me." Do not try to deny or dismiss the anger. At this time you may not be at a place that you want to approach the person or situation that caused the anger. Yet, it is important to see the anger inside of you that needs your attention.

Anger is not a sin. What you do with the anger is a sin, and it is important not to sin when you are angry. Our emotions are present to let us know we have been mistreated. If we do the right thing long enough, our right feelings will follow. Make a choice I am not going to live angry for the next year.

He that is slow to anger is better than the mighty; and he that ruleth his spirit than he that take a city. Proverbs 16:32

Is the situation the problem or how you respond to the situation? Therefore, you can deal with anger constructively in these ways:

- Get God's Word out and study. Get your Bible out and read what the Word says about anger, hurt, frustration and forgiveness. God words are the way, the truth and the life.
- Pray. When you pray for your enemies, you have a hard time being mad with the person who hurt you. Prayer changes things.
- Write it out. Pick up your pen or pencil and begin to write what you are feeling. You don't have to be concerned about whether it makes sense to you. You do not have to worry about the grammar or the spelling. Just continue to write until the anger subsides and you feel an emotional shift inside of you.
- Exercise. Physical exercise is a great way to express anger. When you get mad, minimize stress by moving your body- by walking, dancing, working in your garden or racking your yards.
- Develop a relax response. Be sensitive to the physiological changes in your body during times of anger. When you are angry, your responses increase- your heart beats faster. Deep breathing, meditation and a massage help to relax your body and quiet your mind.
- Role-playing. Johnny cheated on you. You are angry. Imagine Johnny is sitting in an empty chair opposite you. Tell Johnny how his action hurt you. Yell, scream and cry if you want to. Just tell Johnny what is on your mind.
- Keep a journal. Daily record your feelings and experiences and daily review your writings. Pay attention to patterns which allow you to gain insights about yourself.
- Take time-out. When you are angry, you begin to escalate your feelings which can lead to physical or verbal abuse. You can wound others when you are angry. Time-out allows you to prevent escalating- avoiding the anger traps you verbally say to yourself, "I am beginning to get angry and I need to take time out." When you take time out, you leave the situation for at least thirty (30) minutes which will give you time to rethink the situation. Take

time out and just count 1 to 100 or 200 and allow yourself time to cool down and unwind.

- Join a support group. Support groups are an excellent opportunity to talk about your feelings in a network of individuals where you can express yourself freely; knowing that what you say will be respected and kept confidential. Talk about your feelings on a daily basis. Please note that unless you can express your feelings about a negative situation, you will not be able to be in an honest relationship. If you do not know of a support group, ask your family members, friends, your physician or minister for a referral.

Today, you are definitely dealing with a more angry society. You are encouraged to deal with anger. Anger not dealt with produces: unpleasant memories, unresolved conflict, unrealistic comparisons, un-confessed sins, unrealistic expectations, unexpected financial pressures and an uncertain future.

Anger leads to violence and violence leads to conflict. You would not want anger to grow into conflict in your male/female experiences. It is best to be alone than to be involved with individuals who cannot resolve conflict. "You can be alright until Mr. Right comes along."

FORGIVENESS IS POWERFUL AND GENERATES FREEDOM

You thought it was love at first sight, but your intuition told you that this relationship would change everything for the worst. You had a cue but you ignored it. You moved into the relationship blindly, and six months later you are hurt and devastated. You knew he was too charming and too good to be true.

Life is filled with problems. A man/woman that is born of a woman will have a few days and a lot of trouble. You will often find yourself in a problem, just left one or headed for another problem. Throughout life, people will make you mad, hurt you, disappoint you and or disrespect you. Sometimes, it is necessary to let go and let God. Let go and let God deal with the things others did to you.

We all make mistakes. We are all mistaken and sometimes misunderstood. Sometimes, we do wrong things which have bad consequences. Do not be so hard on yourself. This does not mean we can't be trusted afterward.

For all have sinned, and fallen short of the glory of God. Romans 3:3

Forgiveness is not forgetting that someone has hurt you. Forgiveness is about letting go of another person's action(s). Forgiveness does not create a relationship with another person. Unless people speak or acknowledges the truth about what they have done and change their mind and behavior, a relationship of trust is impossible. When you forgive someone, you release them from judgment. Without true change, no relationship can be established.

He healeth the broken heart, and bindeth up their wounds. Psalms 147:3

Forgiveness does not mean you have to trust the one you have forgiven. Forgiveness does not excuse another person's behavior. Forgiveness is a process. You may declare that you have forgiven the man who hurt you fifty times the first, thirty times the second and ten times the third day. One day you will realize that you have forgiven the man that hurt you completely. One day you will pray for the man who hurt you- his wholeness.

Forgiveness has everything to do with relieving oneself of the burden of being a victim and letting go of the pain and transforming oneself from victim to survivor. Do not give your power away to the man who hurt you. The willingness to forgive is a manifestation of spiritual and emotional maturity. Forgiveness of yourself and others allow you love unconditionally.

Happiness breeds happiness. So he cheated on you. So he hit you in your eyes and turned them red. The man tricked or conned you out of $1000. Keep in mind, hurting people hurt other people as a result of their pain. If a man is rude, inconsiderate or abusive, you can almost be certain that he has some unresolved issues inside. He has major problems of anger, insecurity, resentment or heart break he is trying to overcome.

A heart at peace gives life to the body, but envy rots the bones. Proverbs 14:30

The Lord is nigh unto them that are broken heart; and saveth such as be of a contrite spirit. Many are the afflictions of the righteous: but the Lord delivereth him out of them all. Psalms 34: 18-19

Yes, I understand and feel your pain. I have been there and seen that! When a man hurts you, you do not forgive him for his sake. Believe it when I tell you, your forgiveness is for your sake. Can you imagine what the world would be like if the world was filled with people willing to apologize and accept apology? Tell me would the world be a better place if we- men, women, boys and girls - were willing to forgive.

When you hold resentment toward another person, you are bound to that person by an emotional barb wire chain link fence that is stronger than iron. Forgiveness is the only way to dissolve that strong link and get free. If you do not forgive, you are like a prisoner locked up in solitary confinement. You may one day wake up and realize that the prisoner is you. Often in the process of forgiveness, you have to look beyond the person who hurt you-see his fault and see his needs. You will have to confront questions like: Why did he rape me? Why did he pimp me?

It is important to get "stuff" out of you to manage anger. Therefore, you can write about what you are angry about. You can have a conversation with the person you are angry with. You may seek professional help from a counselor or your minister. Forgiveness is a process, but please try to forgive the one who has harmed you. This may be difficult but pray for the one who has harmed you. Try to get to a place where you can love the person for who he is and not who you want him to be. Be aware that you should focus on changing you. You can't change the other person.

Sometimes when we experience negative emotions, we internalize them with self-judgment. It is sometimes important to forgive ourselves. For example, if you were raped on your first date, you may feel dirty, damaged and shame. (1) Recognize the judgments you hold about yourself. (2) List them: I feel dirty; I feel damaged; I feel ashamed. Say aloud that you forgive yourself for those feelings: "I forgive myself for judging myself."

If we would like for God to forgive us for our wrong, sins or mistakes, we should forgive others who have wronged us. True forgiveness is when we get to a place we can thank God for the experience. It is a place of growth that we can see the blessing in adverse situations. We have to ask God the question: God what is in this for me? Forgiveness reflects strength. The weak person can never forgive. Let it go; forgive yourself; forgive the situation; realize that the situation is over and move forward with your life. "You can be alright until Mr. Right comes along!"

But if ye do not forgive, neither will your Father which is in heaven forgive your trespasses. Mark 11:26.

Do Not Be Defeated: There Is Hope

MOMMY UNMARRIED WITH CHILDREN

I know so many single women who have children. Some have been married and many have children and never have met Mr. Right. As a matter of fact, many women say they have never gone on a real date. Much thought has been given to concentrating on whether it is possible to meet a man when you have children.

After my divorced, I was a single mom with the responsibility to raise three beautiful daughters. I was told that no man would want a woman who had three children. The devil tried to deceive me in believing this lie. That is why you have to speak to the devil and tell the "devil you are a lie and I rebuke you in the name of Jesus."

If a man wants you, he will accept your children and you. Children bring about a certain dynamics that has to be viewed through the eyes of realistic lens. If a man is really looking for a serious relationship, it is not the children he will back away from; it is the drama and conditions that come with them. I am sure you have heard about the "baby mommy drama."

Children have fathers who may still be involved in their children's lives which also bring about a level of understanding. If a man senses he will have to get into it with another man over a woman and the kids, he should be inclined to move on to someone he will not need to fight with.

It is best to be honest. Let your potential mate know up front that you have kids and make sure you have handle business with their dad and everything is in order. If a man sees the value of getting involved with you, then he will do just that. If the man feels that three kids are too much for him to deal with, then let him go, and be open for love with someone who will see you and your children as a worthwhile package.

As I stated earlier, when I divorced, I was told no man would want me with three kids. This was never a problem in men wanting to date me. You can meet Mr. Right even if you are married with three kids or more.

Casting down imaginations, and every high thing that exalteth itself against the knowledge of God, and bringing into captivity every thought to the obedience of Christ. 2 Corinthians 10: 5

There will come a time when you will feel it is appropriate for you to introduce your child to the guy you are dating. Arrange for your children and your date to go to a child-friendly place. This will give you an opportunity to observe the man's reaction with you and your children. If your children are older, you may desire to take them on a date and personally introduce them.

Always remember children are a gift from God. You do not have to lock yourself away due the fact that you are a mommy, unmarried with children. Mr. Right can find you. Love will find a way. "You can be alright until Mr. Right comes along."

LOVERS AND THE RECESSION

Money! Money! Money! I hear many people talk about money and how the recession is affecting their lives. The bad economy has soured many good relationships. The bad economy can often make you feel that dating today is impossible.

You may have to alter your dating plans. You may not be able to take your date to a five star restaurant for dinner. The cruise you plan to take to Alaska may have to be placed on hold for the moment. Most women spend much money into dressing, and many would not be caught dead without expensive shoes, purses and accessories. Be willing to make changes if the money is not there. You are encouraged to get your finances in order before looking forward to a future with "Prince Charming."

A guy told me that when he was employed as a college football coach, he could easily spend $300 a week dating. Taking a woman to a restaurant with $20 entrees and $15 for a cocktail was the norm. Taking my date to Broadway shows was not a problem. All this changed when he was laid off and became unemployed. He had to make some changes. He changed from taking out his credit card without looking at the bill. He moved to scanning the menu for the most cost-effective meal. He said each time he did that he felt his manhood slipped away.

He said this was a time of reckoning for him. With his finances in disarray, he became self-conscious about dating that it took months before he felt comfortable inviting a woman on a date. It terrified him to ask a lady to go "Dutch." As the date drew near, he said he felt nervous about whether he had enough money to cover the bill. He was concerned about a woman looking down on him as less of a man because he could not cover the tab for the date.

The lack of money can caused your creativity energy to flow. You will have to think of different ways to date. A date in the park can be romantic. Watching a movie at home and eating popcorn can be enjoyable. Cooking a simple meal for your dinner date can be enjoyable, and he can bring wine and a rose. Agreeing to go "Dutch treat" can be acceptable-each paying his/her bill. A picnic in the park can be romantic and refreshing. Just do not limit and box yourself in.

Some women like to conceal how much money they are making because they feel to reveal that they are the top breadwinner would hurt his feelings. Many sisters believe brothers cannot deal with progressive sisters and would prefer to see women in subservient roles. There are two sides to every story. Many men recognize that women today are on the move and actually feel good to see sisters with a good job. If she is making more money than he is, if she has more titles, that is fine. If she has a company car, that is fine also. If the woman wants to pay for dinner, he feels great that he is having lobster and steak.

The earth is the Lord's, and the fullness thereof; the world, and they that dwell therein. Psalms 24: 1

Let's get honest and communicate. Communication is to a relationship as blood is to life. Women can understand when a man tells her upfront about his limited disposable funds. The reality is a man who has built up his confidence in who he is, what he stands for, and what he is striving for really has no reason to be afraid of a successful woman.

I have heard some sisters say "No money no honey." Women who financial situation is not as they desire do not have to compromise their bodies for money. You do not need a "sugar daddy." You need God. The earth is the Lords and the fullest thereof. All the money in the world is God's money. You are not for sale or resale for that matter. We have to teach our daughters to distinguish the difference between a man who spends money on her and a man who invests in her.

Even in a good economy, money is the lead cause of relationship tension and can fuel arguments. Rich or poor, you have to put money in prospective. As a general rule: Save some; Spend some and Give away some. There are financial fixes you can make, as well as emotional life lines to take to ensure that your relationship and finances not only survive but thrive. You can be alright until Mr. "Right comes along."

Sex, God and You

SEX IN THE USA

We all want to be loved, appreciated and have pleasure and fulfillment in our lives. God gave us the capacity to love and to be loved, to have special friendships. God gave us a sexual nature and sexual desires. Did God give us sex to keep the human race going, or did God give us sex to enjoy oneness with a life partner-for better for worse, for richer of for poor, in sickness and health until death does us apart?

Sex is a beautiful gift from God. In today's society sex sales! Sex is expressed on television, magazines, newspaper, via the internet and yes in our daily conversations. God allows sex as expression of our love in a marriage arrangement.

Sex is like a fire. In the fireplace it can warm your house. To observe fire in the fire place is soothing and can be romantic. If the fire jumps out of the fireplace, we see trouble. The fire can burn your house down. It can kill you.

Flee from sexual immorality. All other sins a man commits are outside his body, but he who sins sexually sins against his own body. 1 Corinthians 6: 18

Even children in the USA are talking about and experiencing sex. Sex is for procreation and not recreation. Too many young and mature individuals are experimenting with sex for pleasure and not purpose.

Sex is now a part of the games people play. Many people use their body to get what they want. I have heard guys say their goal is to get the female to have sex with them the first night they meet. This elevates their ego and they feel like they are the "man."

A mistress confesses she dated married men for years but insisted she was not trying to break up anyone's home. She stated they shared a bond the wives will never understand. She said "I love him so much; there's nothing he can ask me to do sexually that I won't try. He'll never get a "no" answer."

One Brazilian woman expressed that foreign men have told her she is more liberal than women back home. Many brothers who live in the USA are on flight to Brazil as we speak. The Brazilian sister said if she did not enjoy it she would not let it show. She said the most important thing you can do for your man is to compliment him. Tell him that his body is hot and seduce him every day.

Some women get caught up in the concept "by any means necessary." They feel be good to your man and he will be good to you. The party girl says to always act like you are having the most fun in the room. The party girl says men like the fun girl-the one who will dance with them, laugh at their jokes, and not ask too many hard questions.

The stripper acknowledges that some people say that they are sleazy, we are "ho's" and we are "home wreckers." The stripper says this is her job which is designed to entertain high rollers and we know what counts to a man. The stripper lets you know all men like fantasy-the rich and the poor.

Sex is a gift from God. It is not evil. Sex is a powerful gift, and it can be abused and perverted. As a single woman, if you are single, wanting to be married, remember this: it is better to be that way than to be married, wanting to be single. Until you get married, learn to make friends. It is rewarding to get to know people of both sexes. I encourage you to be strong enough to keep sexual activity right out of your relationship until Mr. Right comes along and the date is set. I know this may sound old fashioned, but keep your clothes on with each other if you want to fully enjoy your marriage later.

Many of us rush into sex without getting to know the person, and very often a child is the product of an unhealthy relationship. Many women tend to think that having a baby will make him love me or guarantee he will stay. God created sex to be enjoyed in marriage. A baby is an indication that sex has taken place- not an indication that love was ever there. If he loved you, do you think he would commit to marry you? Just think; God knew the negative effects of sex, and baby mama drama is a big effect. Doing things God's way and staying pure until marriage will help us avoid so much unnecessary drama and give your child a chance- to be raised in a healthy home by a mother and father. A message to the brothers and sisters- if you will not make her your wife, do not make her a mother.

People do not generally expose to the public their valuables. We put our money in the bank. We have to dig deep for oil, diamonds and gold. We hide our expensive jewelry in a jewelry box or a vault. We are careful to protect and preserve our diamonds. Every woman should make a special effort to protect the diamond-between her legs. Your diamond is precious-more precious than rubies and very valuable. Don't give or expose your diamonds to the world. Do not give your diamonds to just anyone-he may not appreciate. Do not flaunt your diamond by dressing too revealing.

Sex is not love and love is not sex. Remember love gives and lust takes. Remember men are like the microwave oven (more instant) and women are like the crock pot (warm up to). Therefore, the "90 Day Rule" may not be long enough. If you concentrate on being the kind of person worth being married to, God will allow Mr. Right to find you. "You can be alright until Mr. Right comes along."

GETTING INTIMATE WITHOUT GETTING NAKED

Everyone longs to give herself or himself completely to someone, to have a deep and committed soul relationship with another, to be loved thoroughly and unconditional. Intimacy means allowing another person the opportunity to "look into me and see." Below are 25 ways to be intimate without getting naked:

1. Tell the Person that you love him.
2. Make him feel loved and respected.
3. Give him a special gift.
4. Compliment him on how great he looks
5. Talk lovingly on the telephone.
6. Make sacrifices for each other.
7. Have a picnic together.
8. Meet each other's family.
9. Go to the library or bookstore.
10. Exercise together.
11. Listen to a favorite CD together.
12. Eat dinner by candle light.
13. Take a drive and go sightseeing.
14. Hide a love note with a love poem
15. Go for a moonlight walk in the park
16. Rent a DVD and watch it while you eat popcorn together.
17. Cook his favorite meal.
18. Send a special card designed by you especially for him.
19. Read a book about love and discuss it.
20. Share a smoothie together.
21. Have your picture taken together and frame it.
22. Make each other a hand crafted gift.
23. Talk about your joy and your pain together.
24. Give him a sexy look.
25. Touch each other in a loving way.

We often associate sex with sexual intercourse. Not enough thought or understanding goes into how special it is to be intimate with someone special. When you are intimate, this becomes the icing on the cake when you are at the place God blesses you to engage in the beautiful act of making love.

Sex is powerful. If you want it, you got to be willing not to have it for as long as it takes, until it comes in a way that is honorable and honoring. Slow it down! You cannot be so desperate wanting someone. You have to develop your own personal, intimate moments so that you are not sex-starved and sex-crazy, and you will know how to say no. It is critical to develop creative ways of nonsexual love and non- verbal expressions of intimacy.

God loves you and not until you discover that only in God is your satisfaction to be found, you will not be capable of the perfect human relationship that God has planned for you. Don't be anxious. Don't worry. "You can be alright until Mr. Right comes along."

Flee youthful lusts: but follow righteousness, faith, charity, peace, with them that call on the Lord out of a pure heart. 2 Timothy 2: 22

CAN YOU LOVE GOD, SEX AND YOURSELF?

Praise the Lord everybody! There is a question I would like to explore with you: How can we achieve moral vision and faith that affirm spiritual nourishment and sexual fulfillment? Women are definitely tied to the two most powerful forces in reality- spirit and sex. However, they seldom think about the essential relationship between spirit and sex. They usually try to establish moral distance between the spirit and sex. Have you seen the manifestation of this in our modern day churches?

About thirty years ago, I was struggling with sex, God and me. I called a minister I trusted for counseling. I told him the issue I was struggling with. His response was: "You are an attractive woman." The way he responded I wondered was he interested in me as a woman. He surely did not give me any advice that I feel assisted me with my struggle.

Daily we witness stereotyped images of women illustrated in extremes like hot, "hoochie-mama" music videos. We rarely see images of long-suffering mothers of the church- and other true voices revealing sexuality and spirituality in our real lives.

How do we address these contradictions? What can the church do to minimize this hypocrisy that exploits female sexuality as it disciplines and condemns it? We need to dispel myths, crush lies, rebuke stereotypes and celebrate the dynamic interaction between spirituality and sexuality.

We are all trying to be Proverbs 31:10 virtuous women but we have this burning in our bodies. This is a reality for many women who are torn between satisfying our desires and living according to the Words of God. Our spirit can be willing but our flesh may be weak. What does this say to women in the church who sit Sunday after Sunday hearing about the things they should not do?

I say we have to get a clearer understanding of what is meant by sexuality. Sexuality has to do with the essential part of who you are, that thing about you which urges you into a relationship, into communion, into creativity-with yourself, with one another, even God. Have you heard the saying "Good girls do not do it?" And if you do, lie about it.

African Americans history goes back to the auction block during slavery. Our bodies were put on display and seen as objects. Men were sold by the size of their chest. Women were sold by the size of their breast, and children were sold by the soundness of their teeth. History about slavery reveals that Black women had to use sex to save their men and families- to keep our babies around and get food to eat. Have you ever thought about how the images we all internalize about our bodies? This resulted in women dealing with stigma, fear and shame. It affects the way we deal with one another even in our male/female relationships. Do we respect our bodies and the bodies of those around us?

Our attitudes about our bodies go back to the Bible. Most preaches (and other individuals called in the five- fold ministry) reflect the Christian tradition in terms of understanding a woman's body only in terms of childbearing and not sexuality. When we discuss the Virgin Mary's birth of Jesus, I have yet to hear in the church the way in which that birth is a very bodily experience. You do not hear about any of the pain and suffering that Mary went through during childbirth.

We recognize that we are sexual beings. How do we express our sexuality without feeling shame and guilt that is often laid upon us in church settings? We are sexually repressed while at the same time we are very sexually active. This hinders our youth and others from express sexuality in life- affirming ways.

I tried to talk to my daughters about sexuality. I am not sure I did the best job in communicating to them. I have learned how to communicate more effective over the years. Even though they are grown and gone from home. I welcome the opportunity to talk with them about anything.

It is difficult to talk about sexuality when our mothers were not comfortable talking about it. As a motivational speaker, I have been blessed to facilitate sessions with many young girls. On several occasion, I have had young girls say to me: "I have this guy I am seeing and I love him. I am beginning to feel like having sex with him." I would reply: "You are wearing a beautiful birthstone ring and a pretty small diamond ring. If this guy asked you for your rings, would you give them to him?" The young girl replies: "I am not going to give him my rings." I emphasized to the young girl: You are going to give this young guy your body. Do you place more value on your rings than you do your body? So you see this is where the problem lies. How do we get women to make the connection and stop selling their bodies cheap (like USDA branded beef) at their spirit's expense?

Building a woman's self-esteem is worth devoting our time and resources. A healthy self-concept leads to healthy expressions of sexuality. If we spend our energy building healthy self-esteems, we would not have to say, "Don't have sex." I encourage young and mature women to protect your "diamonds" -love your bodies. You are the best you have going for you at any time in your life. When we talk about self-esteem, we are talking about our daughters' feeling they are worth being loved so if they are engaging in sex early, they know that this behavior is not consistent with their desired goals of feeling like a worthwhile lovable human being.

If you have been sexually abused, take it to God. Remember everything that concerns you concerns God also-your spirituality and your sexuality. You can take everything to God. He values an intimate and personal relationship with you. God can look at you and love you just as you are. You do not have to feel trapped, isolated, ashamed or alone.

I often listen to Evangelist and Spiritual Teacher Joyce Meyers. She often talks about how her father molested her as a child. What I love about her is her openness in sharing her testimony how God healed her. She shares how she was moved to forgive her dad, take care of him and lead him to Christ before he died.

It is absolutely necessary to create spaces and places where women can feel safe to discuss life issues. The church should be the community hospital where women and men can come in and be healed. You do not have to get dressed up. Each person can come as he or she is.

We cannot act like sex has never been an issue in our own lives. If truth be told, we were not always where we are now. Otherwise, we are living a lie and girls are trying to live up to a standard that nobody could live up to because we did not even live up to it. We have to find ways to have fearless Bible study in churches. We have to open up and really deal honestly with passages in the Bible.

Do we sometimes spiritualize some of the Biblical stories? We are fascinated with poems in the Song of Solomon. What was going on with Solomon was a hot and heavy love affair. We have to be open minded and not afraid to bring out the secular text in the church. Tell me what is wrong with bringing in some of the stuff that our youth are reading, singing, watching and talking about. Why are we afraid to talk about sex, drug, homosexuality, Facebook, sexting, date rape, domestic violence and hip-hop culture? Churches have to open the Bible up in a more honest way.

Yes, it is possible to love God, sex and yourself at the same time. The power is in your choices. Sex is the most powerful experience a human being can have because it reflects creation-procreation. Even beyond procreation the sexual union is the greatest communion one can have with God because it is joining one's self to something higher than even we can experience. It is important to understand that to be a spiritual being is to be a sexual being.

The church engages in spiritual lessons telling people what to do and what not to do. Do not have sex before marriage. Do not masturbate. Do not do this and do not do that. We have so many young and mature people engaging in unsafe sex. We have to refrain from instructing people to say "Just say no; do not have sex." Is sex life enhancing? Is sex before marriage life enhancing? Is sex life enhancing during your teenage years? The big questions: Is sex good for you at this time. I believe if you feel good about yourself, than you are going to make certain choices.

Women should not have sex with anyone if their heart is closed. If the heart is filled with pain and anger, refrain from sexual relationships. If you cannot be opened and vulnerable with someone, why would you want to have sex with that person?

Celibacy is a great choice. Every time you have sex with a person, there is a special covenant made between two individuals. When you sleep with somebody, you are exposed to individuals they have slept with. It is alright to preach this from the pulpit.

For me, the best way I can honor myself is to stay empty until I can find my completion. My completion does not come from sexual relationships. Sex revolves around how I am treated all day-every day. Your soul (mind, will and emotions) yearns for the pleasure and satisfaction of being spiritually and physically intimate with a life partner.

God loves you regardless of who you are or what you have done. God loves you even if you have been raped, used and abused. He knows if you are a virgin or not and He loves you anyway. You do not have to hide from God. God loves your scars, rolls, cellulite, bunions, etc.

It is great to grow to the place where you can develop nonsexual relationships with men. I understand that you do not have to have sex with every man who looks at you in a seductive way. For years, I have lived celibately and I had wonderful nonsexual relationships with men. This is therapeutic and can do miraculous healing.

Sexual healing comes when you find new family members because most of us have been taught some negative information in our families of origin-many dysfunctional families. Many of us have been taught what happens in the house stays in the house and we are instructed not to talk to anybody about it. You cannot heal what you cannot reveal and you can conquer what you are not willing to confront. Sometimes, you have to broaden your image of a family by adopting a new family to tell the truth, let that group affirm and validate your issues and let the healing begin.

Fathers need to be concerned about their relationships with daughters as well as their sons. Many fathers never hugged their daughter, never kissed their daughter or told her he loves her. Many fathers have never been intimate with their daughters. Many men may be frightened with females' biological budding, breasts are coming and menstrual cycle has started.

A few years ago, I was eating in this restaurant and I immediately became fascinated with a father feeding his eight year old daughter ice cream. Wow! This was such a beautiful sight. This father was spending intimate, personal, quality, loving time with his daughter. I vehemently believe every father should schedule and go on dates with their daughters-spend intimate quality time with daughters.

As single women we have to be careful not to confused physical intimacy with love. I went through more than ten years being alone-celibacy and not in a male/female relationship. We are human flesh (sexual) on a spiritual (God) journey. Yes, we can love God, sex and self. I realize that God loves me. God says if we love Him, we will obey him. God continues to bring me through mountain and valley experiences. This is the day that the Lord has made. It is time to celebrate. You are beautiful and valuable to Him. Even if you are not in a relationship, it is alright. "You and I can be alright until Mr. Right comes along."

Is It Okay To Date?

DATING A YOUNGER MAN

Falling in love is a beautiful thing. At one point or another, everyone finds that special someone who makes the heart skip a beat. Almost everyone will go through a few Mr. Wrongs before Mr. Right comes along. When you are attracted to someone, it is not only because of their possible good looks or great personality. Chemistry plays a key role when developing feelings for someone special.

When you meet someone and the chemistry is there, attraction can occur. This can be the case with a younger man. You click immediately. Then you begin to wonder whether age will be an issue. There are young men who feel more compatible with older women who possess qualities they admire.

Despite the statistics, there are plenty men out there. However, too many women have allowed others to decide what makes acceptable husband material- Mr. Right. They reject a potential mate because he comes from a culture different from theirs, or because he has the wrong skin color or social status. Some of us even make height an issue. And, yes, we make age an issue too.

It is interesting that a 45 year old sister probably would not hesitate to date a 55 year old man but would struggle with the idea of dating a 30 year old man. We are somewhat prepared to marry an older man because we may feel he is wiser and will take care of us. Dating and marrying an older man does not solve our relationship problems.

Women should not limit their choices by ruling out younger men. Your decision about whom to love should be based on whether the man is emotionally healthy and loving to engage in a healthy male/female relationship. So what, the man is younger. God does not say you cannot date or marry a younger man. As long as you are not "rocking the cradle" with a minor-underage person and you are equally yoked, do not limit your choices.

We have to spend time putting life in the proper prospective. This is your life and you only get one chance to live life. No one has the right to try and fit you in a box and close it, dictating your happiness. God says he came that you might have life more abundantly. You deserve healthy love. You deserve the best of what life has to offer you. Life is love- love it. If a younger man makes you happy, go for it-wherever you find it. In the meantime, "You can be alright until Mr. Right comes along."

And he said, the things which are impossible with men are possible with God. Luke: 18:27

DATING OUTSIDE MY RACE

Diversity is what makes America great. Our country's cultural groups give the USA spices and richness as reflected in the many ingredients we creatively select in our salads. The world is like a salad made of many ingredients: lettuce, tomatoes, carrots, raisins, onions and much more. The salad ingredients reflect the variety of different ethnic groups: African American, White or European American, Hispanic American, Native American, Asian American, and individuals of mixed races. If we can open our minds, we can date individuals from different walks of life-cultures.

Culture is defined as all that people have learned and shared, including skills, values, language, knowledge, perception, motives, symbols, traditions, religion, etc. Ethnic group is defined as a group of people bound together by common traits which are culturally distinct or unique.

You can expand your pool of available men if you open up your world to date outside your race. I have not seen anything in the Bible which says it is wrong to date another race. As long as you are equally yoked- go for it.

Remember, no one should assume personal guilt for historical events which they had no control. We will not progress by disrespecting or "bashing" of any culture, ethnic group, gender, or other group. Learn to appreciate the similarities and differences in people.

When dating someone from another race or culture, it behooves each of you to understand each other's culture. You and your mate should communicate about cultures. With this diversity in people comes a diversity of norms, values, beliefs, traditions, family, problem solving methodologies and roles of males and females.

You must take risks to open channels of communication in cross-cultural situations. Taking risks means to make oneself opened and vulnerable in taking the first step toward establishing trust. Cross-cultural learning and communication can only take place when both parties have established enough trust to permit some exposure of who they are.

Dating outside your race can be a fascinating experience. We are all special gifts. Some gifts come wrapped in black paper, some come wrapped in white paper, others come wrapped in multi-colored paper. Some gifts come from the United States of America. Some gifts come from Africa, Russia, and Asia. Some gifts come in skinny boxes, some come in fat boxes. Take a few minutes enjoying the wrapping but please so not forget to look inside the box. You would not want to miss this gift. In the mean-time, open your mind and enjoy God's diversity. "You can be alright until Mr. Right comes along."

Every good and perfect gift comes from above, coming down from the Father of the heavenly lights, who does not change like shifting shadows. James: 1: 17

WOMAN DATING A WOMAN

I have been blessed to speak at many prisons. One experience I will never forget was at a women correctional institution. Our focus topic was: "Bridging the gap from prison to home and the community." These ladies were quite open when discussing the "Male/female Experience".

These women told me about the pain they experienced in relationships. Many told me that they would never date or marry a man. They made it clear that they were done with men. Fast forward the clock ten years and I hear women in the community openly talk about their relationships with other women. I see women on the streets holding hands. I see women dressed like men and it is sometimes hard to distinguish if they are male or female.

I beseech you therefore, brethren, by the mercies of God, that ye present your bodies as a living sacrifice, holy, acceptable unto God which is your reasonable service. Roman 12:1

I am not to judge. How do we validate our lesbian sisters' right to live fully despite the homophobic religious narrative? The Bible is clear that homosexuality is not favored by God. This is not a condemnation of our lesbian sisters. We all sin and fall short of the glory of God. You sin, we sin and I sin too.

Homosexuality is viewed as being contrary to nature since God's primary force is life and the re-creation of life. God created everything in pairs including Adam and Eve. One of the primary desires of God was and is to create and re-create.

Thou shalt not lie with mankind, as with womankind: it is an abomination. Leviticus 18: 22

Sex is exciting because it is an act of creation. The physical act of hugging, kissing, and embracing and then the ultimate consummation of the union are the most powerful experiences a human being can have because it reflects creation.

Today, like never before, we are witnessing men and women, young and old, from every culture come out of the closet acknowledging they are gay. Individuals from the lesbian, bisexual, gay and transgender (LBGT) community touch all of our families.

We all sin and fall short of the glory of God. Some of us fornicate, commit adultery, engage in prostitution, some are rapist and some date the same sex-women dating women. God allows us our free and permissive will. God does not hate the sinner (the person); He hates the sin (the sinful act). Whom do you choose to love and obey?

Flee from sexual immorality. All other sins a man commits are outside his body, but he who sins sexually sins against his own body. 1 Corinthians 6:18

If we claim to be without sin, we deceive ourselves and the truth is not in us. If we confess our sins, he is faithful and just and will forgive us of our sins and purify us from all unrighteousness. 1 John 1: 8-9

What to Do When Loneliness Strike?

WHERE IS MR. RIGHT?

As a Premarital Counselor, I often enjoy asking couples, where did they meet. They tell me that "lightning" can occur anywhere. Would you like to meet the man of your dream -Mr. Right? You have to be moving in the mix.

The best way to meet someone is to relax and not be uptight about meeting someone in the first place. When you are just out enjoying life and engaging yourself and going to interesting places, you will definitely meet people. Do not be deceived because no one is going to knock on your door and say, "We understand you in this apartment or house and you are lonely."

You can meet a perspective partner while carrying out everyday activities like jogging, shopping, or gardening. The best place to meet someone is where you are not in a defensive posture. Relax and enjoy! Know yourself and know what you want in a partner. Then place yourself in the location that meets your own needs. You will not meet a mate sitting in front of the TV watching "The Young and the Restless." You have got to get out of your house or apartment.

Think in terms of where men go. Men like their "toys". Men are into repairing and maintaining their cars. Men are into computers. They are also into body, body building, and health food stores.

The 20 Best Places to Meet a Man

1. Work
2. Church
3. Health Clubs
4. Supermarkets
5. Laundromats
6. Homes and parties/picnic of friends
7. Weddings
8. Conferences, Seminars and Conventions
9. Social and Community Organizations
10. Bus Stops, Train Stations, Bus Stations and Airports
11. Class Reunions
12. Sporting Goods Stores
13. Libraries
14. Concerts
15. Internet
16. Cooking, computer, Auto Repair Classes
17. Colleges
18. Sporting Events, Football, Baseball or Basket Ball Game
19. Social Mixing Party
20. Night Clubs, Bars or Social Clubs

By now, I am sure you may be asking: where is the best place to meet Mr. Right? Church is a great place to meet a mate. Night club or bars are considered by many to be the worst place to meet a mate. The internet is not recommended as the best place to meet a mate. Do not limit yourself to meeting someone only on Saturday or Sunday. You can meet a mate wherever you are. "You can be alright until Mr. Right comes along."

WHAT IF MR. RIGHT DOES NOT COME ALONG?

You may feel it has been a long time coming and you start to wonder and ask yourself: Will Mr. Right come along? Is it God's plan, I am not married? My answer is he will come if it is the will of God. If he comes, praises be to the Lord. If he does not come, may it please God Almighty? Until he comes, I say let's be about our Father's business.

One thing for sure, we do not have to look for Mr. Right. Believe me, the type of men who are willing to give love and receive love are all around us. They are on the job, at the gym, at weekly church service, at the mall, at the football game, at the car wash, and at the Technology Conference.

You could meet him at home but just sitting around the house watching Housewives of Atlanta, waiting for the phone to ring may not be the answer. You have got to get up, get motivated and above all have the right attitude. Do not allow man hunting to become an obsession. Do not put your life on hold waiting for Mr. Right. Instead forget about looking for Mr. Right and start pursuing your dreams. When you feel good about yourself, you attract goodness to you.

So, therefore, get the attention of someone who is worthy of you- a man who loves God, a man who is successful, emotional stable, healthy, well rounded and attractive to you. Take time to work on those qualities for yourself. When you value yourself, you teach others how to treat you. If you do not value yourself enough to provide the good things, why should anyone else?

Put the focus on you. When you put the focus on you, there are fringe benefits. The focus on you and not on someone else puts you in control. When you start making great things happen for you, you put yourself in the path of meeting great new people. Some of them may become your friends, business networks, others acquaintances, and you will also create opportunities to meet Mr. Right.

Bloom where you are planted. We have to learn to work with what God has blessed us with. Once Mr. Right is not consuming your mind and your time, the mission becomes possible to meet your soul mate. Get ready to have some fun and expand your circle of male acquaintances.

It does not matter if he does not dress in Armani or drive a fancy Mercedes. Clothes and material trappings do not make the man. First Lady Michelle Obama says when she met President Barack Obama; he was not driving a fancy car. He had a hole in the bottom of his car. He did not have a traditional job. He was not planning to write a book which will become a best seller. Michelle Obama was an attorney at a major law firm making plenty money. President Obama was not even close to being Michelle Obama equal. She says she saw the man instead of judged him by the car he drove. She dated potential. Most women are reluctant to date potential. I am sure she did not know he would one day become the first African American president of the United State of America.

Mr. Right could be singing in the choir right beside you. But you will never know if you do not reach out to get to know him better. One of my friends is 84, and she recently married a man she adores.

Relax. Open your mind and heart. Be open to making new friends and exploring what you have in common. Getting to know a man does not always have to end up with him placing a ring on your finger. Every man God allows you to meet is not for him to be your lover or your husband. He might continue to be you friend who you enjoy hooking up with to just talk. You can find that you enjoy hooking up for pleasure and purpose. This can take much pressure off the relationship.

Do not allow yourself to be closed minded. Yes, you can speak to him first. Think about this. How do you expect to meet someone if you refuse to approach him? Sisters have no problems approaching another sister she does not know. She will not hesitate to ask her: "Girl, where did you get that "bad" red shoe from?" When a guy strikes our attention, we may even refuse to pay him a deserved compliment. This attitude is no way to meet a friend- waiting on him to make the first move. Some men are shy and may appreciate a friendly hello from a woman.

Men may not readily share this with a woman, but he is initially attracted to aesthetics and your attitude. He is eyeing your figure, your hair. Yes, he is wondering how he will introduce you to his buddies. A woman's personality is important to a man. Men also check for the woman who looks like someone he can have a fun time with. Men will observe women to see if they are approachable and if they do not appear approachable and pleasant; he may pass you by and not give you any attention. I was at a club in Atlanta several years ago and this guy said he was interested in this young lady but he was turned when she seems not to want to dance for fear of perspiring and messing up hair. He gave up and dance with another woman.

A young lady met an interesting man while she was cutting her lawn. He asked did she maintain her lawn on an ongoing basis. They started to talk and spent two hours in friendly conversation. Their conversation was so engaging. They changed phone numbers and have been talking every night since they met. Can you approach Mr. Right or are you waiting for Mr. Right to say hello to you first?

Call unto me, and I will answer thee, and shew thee great and mighty things, which thou knowest not. Jeremiah 33: 3

LET'S DO IT!

One is not born a woman, one becomes one. This becoming takes time. We need time to consider. We need time to make the right choices. We need time to be creative. If it is going to be, it is left up to you. Therefore, you are encouraged to be opened minded and try some of the strategies outlined below for your personal growth.

Try throwing a single party in an appropriate location. With a little creativity, you can meet plenty of new brothers. Do not forget to invite old friends.

There is so much work to do in our community:

Get involved in mentoring young girls.

Engage yourself in hobbies you enjoy.

Take a 10-30 minute walk each day.

Play more games and read more books.

Spend more time with people over 65 and under the age of 10.

Eat more foods that grow on trees and plants.

Drink plenty of water and green tea.

Smile and laugh more.

Make peace with your past so it does not interfere with your future.

Do not compare your life with other people's lives. You see their glory but you do not know their story.

Clear clutter from your house, your car and your desk and allow new energy to flow in your life.

Do not take yourself so seriously- no one else does.

No one is in charge of your happiness but you.

Do the right thing.

Live with 3 E's-Energy, Enthusiasm, and Empathy.

Get in some girl time. Create some sweat equity. Catch up with the girls in the gym while you work off those last extra five pounds. Take a culinary course and then use your skills making Sunday brunch for your friends. You can strengthen your relationship while strengthening your community. Spend time as a volunteer at the soup kitchen or the homeless shelter. Spend time getting away on a day trip to the quaint town 25 miles away. This can be all the vacation time you need. While you are there, get yourself a pedicure, explore the gift shops, bookstores and restaurants. You are not too grown for a slumber party. Invite your friends and enjoy yourselves dressed in your favorite pajamas. Reserving some girl time allows women to step away from their everyday role.

Become the greatest lover. Of yourself! Of your body! Instead of waiting on a man's compliments to enhance your self-esteem, learn to appreciate your body by taking care of it. Take a dance class; schedule a massage.

Enjoy the ride. Remember life is not a dress rehearsal. This is not the Wild Adventures or Busch Garden and you certainly do not want a fast pass. You only have one ride through life; so make the most of it and enjoy your ride.

Marriage to Mr. Right is a commitment to one person- hopefully for life. So do not worry, you have been wise to wait on Mr. Right. Between now and when Mr. Right comes, do not panic- relax, and concentrate on who you are and what you want. Stop worrying about where your next boyfriend will come from and start living your life. Chances are you will find that soon out of the desert, Mr. Right will appear.

But if we hope for what we do not yet have, we wait for it patiently. In the same way, the Spirit helps us in our weakness. We do not know what we ought to pray for, but the Spirit himself intercedes for us with groans that words cannot express. And he who searches our hearts knows the mind of the Spirit, because the Spirit intercedes for the saints in accordance with God's will. Romans 8:25-27

Live life! Make a list of the things you always wanted to do and set about doing them. Life is what happens whether you meet Mr. Right or not. You and your dreams are too important.

"YOU CAN BE ALRIGHT UNTIL MR. RIGHT COMES ALONG."

Ms. Right Is Alright!

WOMANHOOD 101

I hope this book has served as a gentle admonition that each of you might see yourself just a little bit clearer as you strive to seek the better parts of life. Writing this book has truly been a labor of love. It is my desire that you have grown and is ready for Womanhood 101. I hope and pray that this book will assist girls to maturate in the right order: girlhood, womanhood, wifehood and motherhood.

When I was a young girl, I use to sing in the St. Mary Missionary Church choir. I must admit that often I would sing songs that I was just going through the motion. The songs did not have full meaning in my life.

Melodies from heaven began to rain down on me. The following songs came alive in my life. Listen to the lyrics of the following songs:

- Jesus is a way maker. One day He made a way for me.
- I got a new walk and a new talk. I looked at my hands and my hands looked new.
- Sweet Hour of Prayer
- He got the whole world in His hands.
- Praise God from whom all blessings flow.
- He is on the main line tell Him what you want.
- Nothing but the blood of Jesus
- He may not come when you want him, but He is right on time.
- Amazing grace how sweet the sound
- Lift Him up and He will draw all men unto Him

- Been tried in the Fire
- He is a battle-ax in the time of the storm
- I feel better since I laid my burdens down
- He is an on time God-yes He is.

As I grew older and as I grew in Christ, my relationship with God intensified. The old familiar songs helped me to go through mountain and valley experiences. These songs helped to keep my spirit high. Lately I have been singing: "I looked all over I could not find nobody. Nobody greater than you (God and Jesus). I looked high and I looked low and still could not find nobody greater than you."

When I was a child, I spake as a child, I understood as a child, I thought as a child: but when I became a man, I put away childish things. 1 Corinthians 13:11

When I was a young girl, my schedule was wide-open and I use to wait for the guy to call me and make plans. My life revolved around being ready and available for this young man. When I grew up as a woman, I made my own plans and moved forward to achieve my agenda and would tell the guy where he fits in.

When I was a young girl, I tried to control the man in my life. When I grew up to be a woman, I learned that if the man is truly for me, he does not need controlling. I learned if he does not want to be with me, I cannot make him stay. If he wants to stay, no one can take him away from me.

When I was a young girl, I would sit by the phone and wait to see if he had called. If he did not call, I would definitely put him in check. When I grew up as a woman, I was too busy to realize that he had not called.

When I was a young girl, I was actually afraid to be alone. When I grew up to be a woman, I learned it is healthy and productive to sometimes be alone. As a woman, I learned to master my time, using my time for personal growth and development.

When I was a young girl, I ignored the good guys because I did not know any better. When I grew up to be a woman, I learned the difference between men with positive and negative qualities. I learned to ignore the bad guys.

What a big reality shocker: When I was a young girl, I thought a female had to make a man come home. When I grew up as a woman, I learned that woman makes a man want to come home.

When I was a young girl, I spent a lot of time worrying about whether I was pretty and good enough for this man. When I grew up to be a woman, I began to appreciate that I am pretty and good enough for any man.

When I was a young girl, I tried to monopolize all of the guy's time demanding to know where he was at all times- did not want him to be with his friends. When I grew up to be a woman, I learned to realize that a little bit of space makes the time together more special.

When I was a young girl, I use to think a guy's crying is considered weak. When I grew up to be a woman I learned that a man was not a man until he could cry. A woman can offer him a tissue and still love him.

When I was a young girl, I wanted to be spoiled and would expect expensive gifts on birthday, Valentine and Christmas. I yearn for his time and attention. When I grew up to be a woman, I could show him love and make him comfortable enough to reciprocate without fear of him losing his manhood or me losing my womanhood.

When I was a young girl, I would get hurt by one man and make all men pay for it. I would take excessive baggage to the next relationship. When I grew up to be a woman, I learned that this hurt was as a result of one man.

When I was a young girl, I would fall in love and chase aimlessly after love in the wrong places, ignoring all signs and red flags of a bad relationship. When I became a woman, I learned that the one you love may not be Mr. Right.

If you are still single, reflect on the extra privileges and responsibilities to serve God with undivided attention. Oftentimes, we miss the point that when we are married much time is spent on how to please our husband or how to please the world. Do not get me wrong. There is nothing wrong with pleasing your husband. However, I think we often forget how wonderful it is to have much time to please God.

Rev. R.B. Holmes once stated: "You cannot try to prepare folks to get to heaven and not deal with the hell folks are undergoing down here." I am reminded that if you knew better you would do better. I hope this book has helped to prepare you do be alright until your change comes.

It is my desire that your wants are lining up with God's will for your life. When your will and God's will become one, miracles and favor manifest in your life. I hope darkness has been dispelled and you are now moving to the marvelous light. You cannot teach what you do not know. I will be grateful if the information outlined in this book has moved you to become more powerful and you have gained a greater understanding. With increased knowledge and wisdom, you can now reach and teach others.

Growing to be a woman is a process. I hope you have learned much reading this book. I believe you have passed the course Womanhood 101. You are now ready for the next chapter in your life. I know the best is yet to come. I hope you are now saying "I can be alright until Mr. Right comes along."

SISTER TO SISTER: THANK YOU

I know sometimes we are experiencing so much. Some days are joyous, but many days we experience so much gloom and hardship. We know how special and important it is to have a special man in our life. However, reality shines a bright light in our lives daily saying do not give up. Keep the faith! I have said so many times "You can be alright until Mr. Right comes along. He may come today, tomorrow or never.

You are winner when you prepare yourself to receive the love you deserve. I am sure you ask the questions. Will Mr. Right come? How long will it be before Mr. Right comes? Sister to sister, I say take a leap of faith by believing. Believe in yourself. A new chapter in your life is waiting to be written.

If you could carve out the life for yourself that reflects living the most fulfilling, joyous, creative and adventurous quality of life, what would it be? What changes would you make? Would your life reveal you are enjoying life married, committed or being alright until Mr. Right comes along?

I am sure most women desire to meet Mr. Right. However, you have got to be willing to be by yourselves for the rest of life if necessary. You have to learn to be true to your God- centered self- doing what brings you joy. Do what brings you joy and the right brother will show up if it be the will of God.

Just because Mr. Right does not show up in your path next week, please do not freak out. Please be patient and realize that sometimes you may suffer and go through desert experiences along the way. God timing is not our timing.

Therefore, do not put God on your timetable. True love or Mr. Right can come at 50, 60, 70, or 80 years of age. There is no age limit after which you or your friends can say you will never get married. I am sure you have heard the saying "age is nothing but a number." Another saying is "nothing gets old but your clothes". A few months ago, one of my friends who is eighty plus years of age informed me that she married last year.

You are encouraged to move to a loving place. When you moved to a place of love, you do not have to live with him, sleep with him and have his babies too. Give the man space so he can explore the possibility of a committed relationship.

Be aware of the man who wants you to ride in the car with him that has three tires on it. Get ready for a bumpy ride. One tire is flat or something has happen to it. If you want to make cheese cake, you have to know what ingredients to purchase, then mix and bake. If you want cheese cake, do not settle for muffins.

Most of us have no problem receiving love but giving love becomes an issue. Many times we fantasize about receiving love but many of us fear giving love. If you run into a love giver, you will always see a crowd. Imagine someone standing on Main Street passing out $100 bills. He/she would have a crowd around him. When the $100 is no longer available, the crowd would disappear.

Some of us give "feeling good" the same effects of love. He is great in bed. He makes me feel like a queen. But when we add unconditional love in the equation, we see how starved we are. I am talking about love which is present not if, when or because he does. I am talking about him loving you in spite of it all. When this man shows up, you know he is Mr. Right and there is no question about him.

A man is known by the fruit he bears. Ask him: What do you want in life? Where do you see our relationship going? Where do you see yourself in five and ten years? What is your vision? How do you deal with conflict?

Sister to sister, it is important that we love each other. When a man talks negative about my sister(s), it gives me a check in my spirit. Sometimes, sisters can be competitive, jealous and darn right mean to each other. There are sisters who feel superior to other sisters because of materialism and classism. We have a hard times sometimes empowering each other.

Empowering other sisters is important for us to do because it influences men and enhances their perception of sisters.

We will all have some hardships in our lives. There is a possibility that we will experience hurt, defeat, loneliness, divorce and yes, sometimes, depression at some point in our lives. Let's not judge. If you have not seen any "rain" in your life, just hang around for a while. You will see sometimes rain and sometimes storm. Just hold on; you will see the calm after the storm and you can also grow in faith as a result of God taking care of you.

Sisters, let's stay anchored in God. Let us not allow arrogance, disobedience, denial, rebellion, ego, lack of repentance inflict us with wounds which prohibit us from being all we need to be in our works with God.

The world is nothing but a school of love. Each day you wake up, you wake up to "Life University." Our relationships with our friends, family and associates are the university in which we are meant to learn what love and devotion truly are.

The human state is not about being perfect. We are in this life to learn and grow. We do best by finding God's plan for us and following it. Life is by no means easy. Yet by growing, overcoming and experiencing transformation, this can be one of life's greatest joys.

Let's not emasculate (weaken) our man by crushing him with hard words and negativity. Let's not try and do too much for a man. You cannot buy his love. Women who believe that a man's dependency will translate into love and a permanent relationship are making a mistake. Women who develop the "mothering" vehemently believe dependent men will always need and love them. Yes, mothering men will move them to need you but love you-no. The truth is a male who is "mothered: will eventually need to detach, to become independent and transition away from mommy.

Sister to sister, I want you to become vividly aware that you possess all the inner strength, wisdom and creativity needed to make your dreams come true. This is often hard for most of us to realize because the source of personal power is buried beneath our monthly bills, deadlines, household chores, our family and our male/female relationships.

We have lost touch with our inner resources. We have bought into the flawed conclusion that our peace and happiness come from external events, people, things and places. Therefore, we learn to rely on circumstances outside ourselves. We do not have to do this any longer. We know through God all things are possible. We have put our life in the proper perspective.

I know there have been times that you wanted the storm in your life to cease. I know there have been times you desired God to change the situation. Could it be that God has not changed the situation because He is trying to change you?

The best use of life is to love. The best expression of love is -would you believe - time. The best time to love is now. Sisters, I love each of you! You have blessed me and I pray this book is a blessing to you, your daughters, your sisters, aunts, nieces and yes your brothers, fathers, sons and Mr. Right too. "We can be alright until Mr. Right comes along." When Mr. Right does come along, I hope you can say, "It was well worth the wait."

Before I say "I do"

Making a decision about who you will say "I do" to is one of the most important decisions you will make in your life. Try to "act with knowledge." Proverbs 13:16 say:

Every prudent man dealeth with knowledge; but a fool layeth open his folly.

As one lady put it, "you really cannot love a person until you get to know him." Before offering your heart to someone and saying "I do", pay attention to what he does and how he speaks. Observe how he treats people.

It is necessary to take time to observe and get the answer to important questions. Getting to know someone in this way takes time and patience. But it will enable you to see attitudes, traits, habits and qualities that will either confirm your feelings or cause your feelings and behavior to change before you say "I do."

Even a child is known by his doing, whether his work be pure, and whether it be right. Proverbs 20:11

Yes, sooner or later his actions will reveal who he is on the inside. However, it behooves you to make an assessment of who he is before you say "I do." This is no time to resort to a "tricky tongue" or false flattery.

Deliver my soul, O Lord, from lying lips, and from a deceitful tongue. Psalms 120:2

Please exercise sound judgment and make a personal assessment of you and your mate's relationship before you say I do. This is a wise assessment to make before you make a commitment for better –for worse; for richer-for poor; in sickness and in health until death due you apart.

Slow down the process and ask the right questions. You do not need to be anxious for nothing. You have been alone for a certain period of time. You need to know who you are connecting to. It is also advisable that he knows who you are also. Information is the power you need to empower yourself.

Confidentiality and privacy are of utmost important. Before you say I do, please explore answers to the following questions:

Before You Say I Do Take a Look at Spiritual/Ethical Values:

1. What are your/his spiritual values?
2. Are you a born again Christian?
3. Are you following Christ?
4. Are you committed to biblical problem solving?
5. Are we equally yoked spiritually?
6. Do you have an intimate and personal relationship with God?
7. Does spirituality play a role in our male/female relationship?
8. Are you opened to spiritual counseling prior to marriage?
9. What religion denomination do you worship or belong to?
10. Do you expect me to join your church or attend church with you?

Before You Say I Do Take a Look at Family values:

1. What are your spiritual values?
2. What is the structure of your/his family (mother, father, siblings etc.)?
3. Are you adopted?
4. Have you lived in a foster home in the past?
5. Did you experience problems in your family in the past?
6. Can you communicate effectively with your family members?
7. What is your relationship with your mother?
8. What is your relationship with your father?

9. What is your relationship with your brother(s) and sister(s)?
10. Are there any issues which are unresolved with your family?
11. Are there issues that we need to discuss with your family?
12. Did your family experience any dysfunctional behavior(s)?
13. Do you have a positive relationship with your parents?
14. Do you have children by other women and what are your responsibilities?
15. What is your vision for our future family?

Before You Say I Do Take a Look at Finances:

1. How important is money in marriage?
2. Are you willing to develop a financial statement?
3. Are you willing to assist in developing a family budget?
4. Would you prefer an individual or joint bank account?
5. Should we develop a prenuptial agreement?
6. Are you able to provide for a wife?
7. What are your beliefs about a wife pursuing her career?
8. What personal goals have you set regarding your financial preparation for marriage?
9. Have you ever filed bankruptcy? What chapter? When do you expect full relief?
10. Do you have financial responsibility for children? How many? What is the amount of your child support obligation? Annually? Monthly? Weekly? Other?
11. Do you have any financial obligation in terms of paying alimony?
12. Should our family budget be shared with our children?
13. Who will pay for the wedding? Honeymoon?
14. How important is it for us to teach our children about financial empowerment?

Before You Say I Do Take A Look at Civil Reputation:

1. Have you ever been arrested? When? For What?
2. Have you ever been convicted of a crime? What crime? When? What was your punishment? Are you still on probation, parole or community control?
3. Do you still have fines or restitution to pay? How much?
4. Have you ever used drugs? What type of drugs have you used? Have you sold drugs at any time in your life?
5. Have you spent time in prison? When? Where? For what reason?
6. Did prison life hurt, help or rehabilitate you?

Before You Say I Do Take a Look at Your Sexuality:

1. What are your views concerning sex and marriage?
2. Are you living and exercising sexual misconduct in this present relationship?
3. Have you sought and or received restorative counseling and prayer regarding areas of sexual misconduct?
4. Are you currently dedicated to a committed relationship?
5. Have you been sexually active since you accepted Christ as your Lord and Savior?
6. How long has it been since you had sexual intercourse? Have you repented?
7. Have you been a victim of rape or molestation?
8. Have you been involved in incest? Were you the victim?
9. Have you ever indulged in homosexual practices?
10. Are you bisexual?
11. Woman, have you had an abortion?
12. Are you sterile or impotent, man?
13. Are you a virgin?
14. Do you masturbate?
15. Do you have any medical difficulties, disability or disease which will affect sexual intercourse?
16. Is your spouse aware of any concerns or problems you may have regarding your sexuality?

17. Have you sought medical advice or medical attention for physical problems?
18. Are you experiencing menopause at this time?
19. How comfortable are you about abstinence before marriage?

Before You Say I Do Take a Look at Your Mental/Physical Health:

1. Are you experiencing any health issues at this time? Physical? Mental? Emotional? Social? Spiritual?
2. What is your family medical history?
3. Have you been tested for AIDS?
4. Do you experience erectile dysfunction?
5. Have you been tested for sickle cell?

Before You Say I Do Take a Look at Yourself:

1. What are my personal values?
2. What qualities do I have that will help me contribute to a successful marriage?
3. Do I possess the maturity needed to support a mate through difficult times?
4. Am I committed to make a lifetime commitment to my mate?
5. Am I mature and past the youthful age when sexual feelings run strong and can distort my judgment?
6. Do I keep calm under pressure or do I give in to uncontrolled expression of rage?
7. Is my personality cheerful and happy or am I predominately gloomy and pessimistic?
8. Am I intimidated by my mate's association with male or female friends?
9. How will you deal with outside children or relationships?
10. What do you see as the role of the husband and the wife?
11. How do you resolve conflict?
12. How do you handle undesirable behavior of your mate?
13. What are your views and feelings about alcohol and other drugs?

14. What can you share with your partner that your partner will not observe by looking at you?
15. Can you cook? Do you enjoy cooking?
16. If you could write your wedding vows, what would your vows be?
17. How do you honestly feel about your mother or father?
18. Why do you want to get married?

Before You Say I Do Take a Look at Your Partner:

1. What type of character does he/she have?
2. What type of reputation does he/she have?
3. What type of morals does he/she have?
4. How does he/she treat me?
5. How does he treat members of his/her family?
6. How does he/she handle temptations?
7. Is he/she over previous relationships?
8. Does he/she bring "excess baggage" to the relationship?
9. What are his/her short range goals? Long range goals?
10. Does he/she desire children?
11. What is his/her family like?
12. Does he/she have unresolved family issues?
13. Does he/she show you that he/she loves you?
14. Does he/she share the same thoughts or vision for the future together?

Before You Say I Do -Take a look at Previous Marriages:

1. Is the divorce final? When?
2. Why did the previous marriage(s) end?
3. Has there been repentance?
4. Has there been forgiveness?
5. Were there attempts toward reconciliation?
6. Has he/she made restitution to the former spouse?

Before You Say I do Have You Received Parental Consent?

1. Do you have consent of your natural parents?
2. If appropriate, do you have consent of you adopted parents?
3. Do you have consent from your spiritual parents (the persons responsible for your spiritual well- being like your pastor, God-Parents, legal guardian etc.)?

Thanks to Metropolitan Cathedral of Praise Church, Havana, Florida for sharing the marriage assessment tool stated above.

Peace I leave with you, my peace I give unto you: not as the world giveth, give I unto you. Let not you heart be troubled, neither let it be afraid. John 14:27

You are encouraged to stay in the favor of God. The favor of God will take you places that your knowledge, skills, ability, contacts or money will not. Always remember what you do in secret, God will reward openly.

The favor of God is giving you supernatural increase. The favor of God will produce restoration of everything that the enemy has taken from you. Whatever has happen to you (positive or negative), ask God to make you better and not bitter.

God is producing favor in front of your enemies. God's Favor is producing great victory in what seems to be great impossibilities. The favor of God is producing increase in your assets. Favor is producing recognition and preferential treatment for you right now. The favor of God is winning battles for you that you do not have to fight. Mr. Right is on his way!

The Best is Yet to Come!